URZIDAL, Johannes. **There Goes Kafka**, tr. by Harold A. Basilius. **Wayne State, 1969 (c1968). 231p il 68-21544. 7.95**
A welcome addition to the growing list of works on Kafka from writers who belonged to the Prague circle of Kafka's friends and acquaintances, e.g. Max Brod and Gustav Janouch. This is not a Kafka monograph, nor an interpretation of Kafka's works, but rather an interesting and successful attempt, based on personal experiences and recollections and a personal friendship with Kafka, to recreate and interpret the atmosphere and spirit unique to Prague which permeates all of Kafka's writings. Included are portraits of people close to Kafka, commentaries on Kafka's relation to the plastic arts and on his relation to his own Jewish heritage and the German speaking Jewish milieu of Prague, remarks on the influence of Edison on Kafka and the latter's admiration for the "Wizard of Menlo Park," as well as an abridged version of the eulogy, long thought lost, delivered by Urzidal on the occasion of the memorial service held in 1924 shortly after Kafka's death. Basilius has produced a very readable translation, but one which cannot completely deny its German original.

CHOICE   S

Language & Litera

Germanic

Professor Johannes Urzidil was born in 1896 in Prague. After completing his philosophical studies there, he became one of the younger poets of the German expressionist movement and was in close contact with the Prague Literary Circle of Brod, Kafka, Werfel, and others. In 1939 he emigrated to the United States via Italy and England and settled in New York, where he is still living. His first publication was a volume of expressionistic poems (1919). Professor Urzidil has published seven volumes of stories and novels and is the author of many essays and treatises. Among his better known and more important scholarly works are *Goethe in Böhmen (Goethe in Bohemia)*, 1962; *Goethes Amerikabild (Goethe's Image of America)*, 1958; and *Amerika und die Antike (America and Ancient Antiquity)*, 1964. He was awarded the Swiss International *Prix Veillon* for the best German novel (1957), the literary prize of the City of Cologne (1964), the Great Austrian State Prize for Literature (1964), and the Andreas Gryphius Prize (1966). He is a corresponding member of the German Academy of Language and Poetry in Darmstadt, of the Austrian Adalbert Stifter Institute, and of several other learned and literary societies. Works of Johannes Urzidil have been translated from the German originals into English, French, Italian, Czech, Dutch, Hungarian, Russian, and Spanish.

^{BY} JOHANNES URZIDIL

TRANSLATED FROM THE GERMAN BY

HAROLD A. BASILIUS

Wayne State University Press   Detroit   1968

THERE GOES

Franz Kafka

KAFKA

This book is the authorized English translation of *Da geht Kafka,* enlarged edition. Deutscher Taschenbuch Verlag, GmbH and Co., KG, München. © Copyright 1965 Artemis-Verlag-AG, Zürich, Switzerland.

Sketch of Franz Kafka by Hans Fronius. (Photo, courtesy, The Bettmann Archive, New York.)

CONTENTS

TRANSLATOR'S NOTE

All translations of Kafka's statements or writings are my own unless otherwise specifically indicated.

I have tried to incorporate into the translation as much as possible of the flavor of Professor Johannes Urzidil's exciting though highly personal German style. Urzidil's characterization of Kafka's style (see page 42) seems to me also an excellent description of his own style, viz.: "The style [of *The Next Village*] . . . is the characteristic Kafka-like

7

interminable sentence containing parenthetic digressions and seeming never to want to end. Like life itself which it comprehends, this sentence is labyrinthine and at the same time lucid, abstract yet concrete, a realistic determination without pathos. It is full of reservations and elaborations just like the world itself. . . ." [Gerhard Trapp's *Die Prosa Johannes Urzidils*, Berne, 1967 deals extensively with Urzidil's style(s).]

As all other languages, so German, of course, also has its share of words and phrases for which there are no precise counterparts in English. Hence, I have rendered *Dichter* in the specific sense as "lyric poet" but in the generic sense as "literary artist." *Geist* I have translated with "spirit-intellect-will," thus combining the intuitive, the cerebral, and the conative. I have used "plastic arts," contrary to the German use of *plastisch*, to designate collectively the arts of painting, sculpture, architecture, etc.

I should like to make grateful acknowledgment to John Murray of London for permission to quote the eightieth aphorism of Lao-tse from J. J. L. Duyvendiak (trsl.), *Tao Te Ching* (a component of the series *Wisdom of the East*).

H. A. B.

FK

IN THE PRAGUE
OF EXPRESSIONISM

How did it come about that in the first and
second decades of this century German literature could flourish in Prague, of all places,
with so much power and originality? What
aggregate of vital forces played a part in this
creative and literary milieu? I ought to know
the answers because I was born and grew up
there, and I was a witness as well as a par-
ticipant in that German intellectual world of
Prague, full of universal ideas, ever new
forms, and ethical enthusiasms. But a quick

and unambiguous judgment about the reasons for this phenomenon is impossible. Furthermore, the social, biological, and other assumptions rooted in the material universe can be useful only in part. Such a phenomenon as the congregation of a startlingly large number of significant creative personalities, frequently of the highest rank, within a relatively short period of time and within the narrow confines of a city (just as earlier in Weimar or in Concord) must always remain something sublime and metaphysical. Most of the German authors in Prague were Jews, but their feelings as members of a minority group emerged only on occasion. Their German-language consciousness determined their sense of history more strongly than their descent was ever able to do: (I am using concepts here which were compellingly adduced by the Prague philosopher Felix Weltsch in his study of Kafka). My approach may enjoy a certain corroboration, however incomplete, by virtue of the notion of structure or structural quality (*Gestaltsqualität*), an idea conclusively developed by my teacher Christian, Baron of Ehrenfels and later by Max Wertheimer of Prague. This idea more than anything else provides an ability to recognize the secret of a literary physiognomy, whose disparate individual characteristics become fused into a totality of beauty that does not lend itself to analysis.

The German literary artists and writers of Prague had simultaneous access to at least four ethnic sources, viz., to the Germans to whom they were related by culture and language, to the Czechs who surrounded them in everyday life, to the Jews who historically served as a basic and pervasive factor of the city, and finally to the Austrians, among whom they were born and raised and with whom they shared a common destiny, regardless of whether they viewed this destiny positively or critically. Each of these sources, in turn, derived their respective dynamics from two spheres, namely, the staid, aboriginal inhabitants of the city of Prague and the centripetal surge of the Bohemians. The Bohemians comprised, in part, recent settlers in Prague, and in part also Sudeten-Germans who were attracted to the German University in Prague. Also included were a nucleus of Czech peasants and their descendants gravitating to the provincial, later the state, capital, as well as landed Czech and German Jews from the country who as lesser landowners or lessees represented a unique group. Finally, there was the native Bohemian Austrian nobility, some of them original Czech aristocrats, some of them Austro-Germans, but all of them

11

characterized by a monarchical Austrian orientation. These nobles had palaces in the city as well as imposing country estates throughout Bohemia. Their origins reached far back in time, in some cases as far back as the thirteenth century and the Přemyslide kings. Thus, even the Habsburgers seemed to some of these Czech nobles like relatively recent arrivals. All of the foregoing factors became cumulative, and a literary artist was confronted with this accumulation. As a consequence he removed quickly from a locally circumscribed atmosphere to a larger and more fundamental one.

Czech literary artists and writers, most of them still deeply immersed in their national struggle for survival, could not, however, surrender themselves so easily to that kind of fundamentalism, though indications of it were appearing in the writings of the brothers Josef and Karel Čapek and in the works of a number of plastic artists and musicians striving for universal recognition, in short, in works whose form was calculated to achieve most quickly and directly an artistic world-status though retaining the national stigma. For this reason the personal relations of the German literary artists and writers of Prague to Czech painters and musicians was more viable than their relations to Czech writers.

The grotesque nature of the language barrier also contributed to this situation. Not all German literary folk in Prague had a good command of the Czech language (except for several Jews among them), and only a few of the Czech authors could or wanted to speak German.

For the German writers of Prague, the occasionally friendly, but mostly politically turbulent and brawling symbiosis and interaction, not entirely free of anti-Semitic coloration on the part of the Czechs, this glowing of the alchemistic melting pot of Prague, constituted the prime cause of an unrestricted literary spirit which rapidly created its own literary expression on all levels and for which the movement known at that time as expressionism provided a powerful means of release. For Prague by means of its rich national, social, and religious facets did in fact present them with the spiritual potential of a universal megalopolis, much more brilliant than many a larger European metropolis.

An independent German-language literature had indeed formerly existed in Prague and we can clearly discern its roots by pursuing Goethe's relation to Bohemia and the subsequent efforts of the "Forty-eighters" as well as those of the slightly younger literary artists of the "liberal era," who in the persons of Friedrich Adler and Hugo Salus even extended over into my own youthful development. Rilke also owed a debt to that "liberal era," though he was the leader of the escape of Prague German writers into the European theater of thought, feeling and activity. The epoch whose productions subsequently achieved through Kafka and Werfel a universal acceptance under the decisive influence of Max Brod dates back to Rilke. That sort of thing never before resulted from Prague though during the entire nineteenth century German was so extensively spoken there that the Golden Capital of the Czechs with its hundred towers was regarded superficially by the uninformed almost as a German city, a misinterpretation which was later to have bitter consequences.

Rilke had experienced the Czech milieu at second remove through the people themselves. "The folkish Czech melody" (*"Böhmisches Volkes Weise"*) resounded in his ears and may have provided him with many a word-form or the turn of a sentence. That is a destiny from which no man can or should exclude himself, for it represents a personal enrichment. But in time Rilke turned away from Prague. He had lived all too briefly with the people and the events of the city and country, had shared their woes and good fortunes all too little. But all this would not apply to writers such as Paul Leppin, or Franz Werfel, or Paul Kornfeld, or Max Brod, or Felix Weltsch, the philosopher, or the religiously sophisticated Hugo Bergmann, or Willy Haas, the critical mentor, or Erwin Egon Kisch, the "crazy reporter (*rasender Reporter*)." Obviously all this would apply least of all to Franz Kafka, in whom Prague abode just as Zürich did in Keller or Concord in Thoreau. All the inhabitants of Prague I have mentioned lived with the city, owed her their best, became witnesses of the growing political vehemence of the Czechs, of the gradually declining vitality of the Habsburg monarchy, but also and at the same time in the area of German literature, of which they were spiritual co-inhabitants, they witnessed the liberation of the powers of literary expression from the residues of the Baumbach era of liberal doggerel. In the midst of this revolutionary process they could be more supernational precisely in Prague than anywhere else in the German countries.

By virtue of language as well as atmosphere they had direct access to the great Russians. I, for example, read Tolstoy and Dostoevsky not only in German translation but also in Czech. Hence, I could comprehend these authors not only by virtue of reason but also from common heartfelt linguistic relationships. Modern Czech painting, radically and heroically avant-garde, opened up broad vistas toward France. The enormous natural musicality of the Czechs surrounded us, and the best evidences of the Wagnerism cultivated in Prague but now already in decline were being surpassed by the works of a new musical epoch under the leadership of the Austrian Alexander von Zemlinsky, the teacher and brother-in-law of Schönberg. Of course, we neither could nor wanted to withdraw from the influences of Gerhard Hauptmann and Frank Wedekind in the drama, or from those of Stefan George and Hugo von Hofmannsthal in lyric poetry, and yet the German literary part of Prague remained an autochthonous, indeed, a spiritually autarchic world, which by way of example no longer really understood and indeed completely rejected a Karl Kraus, writing from Vienna though he was a native of Central Bohemia.

However, the sentimental magic of Prague, which once caused the verses of Adler and Salus to resound with Gothic and Baroque wizardry, could no longer provide relief for the artistic emotions of the German expressionists living there. They were attracted instead by the close realistic aspects of life, the continuous flux, wherein the godhead resides (Goethe), the social, the humane and world-friendly (Werfel), the totally European, toward which precisely this city of never-ending aggressive antitheses provoked challenges by the hour. This being the case, the German writers of Prague were a much more supranational lot than the Czechs, bound by nationalist sentiments, or the Sudeten-Germans out in the country. [I edited a literary journal for a while and called it simply *Man* (*Der Mensch*). It was intended to be a general universal platform for German and Czech writers. It lasted only a short year, for "what achievements by man could have lasting value?" (Goethe)]

Prague was a city of raconteurs, of magical realists, of the narrator with a precise imagination (Goethe: *exakte Phantasie*). It is true that Werfel was a widely heard lyrical herald, and the ethically reputable Rudolf Fuchs, a pure and profound lyricist. It is equally true that Paul Kornfeld was one of the protagonists of the German expressionistic drama. But the most far-reaching and decisive literary achievements were attained in the German prose of Prague. This prose penetrated most effectively far out into the world, for it was completely free of any restricting provincialism and commanded the broadest vistas, a prose in which before long those writers also participated who had been attracted to the magnetic field of Prague from the outside, novelists such as Ernst Weiss, Hermann Ungar, and Ludwig Winder (all three, Moravians), Oskar Baum or Melchior Vischer (both from Inner Bohemia). In the Prague of that day they became exponents of the demands for general spiritual freedom of man and of the world.

Today as I recall that Prague it seems to me in essence a Kafkaesque city. This may seem self-evident and almost trivial nowadays but I, and not only I, felt that way already when Kafka was still there among us in Prague. Although Prague is reflected in Kafka's work at best only in occasional paraphrase, it nonetheless pervades all of his writing just as salt pervades the water in that Buddhist parable. Though the salt as such is not visible, the water tastes thoroughly salty. In precisely the same way one can document the immanence of Prague in every character, every situation, and every description from Kafka's pen. A single example: Following the publication of *The Metamorphosis,* Kafka remarked to my father-in-law Professor Karl Thieberger during a casual meeting on the street: "What do you have to say about the dreadful things happening in our house?" This might seem funny to anyone not knowing Kafka. It was irony, to be sure, as most everything was to Kafka, but not only irony. It was also serious realism.

At the time of Kafka's major productivity, Prague was most typically Prague and also most typically Kafkaesque. The actual essence of that city can be grasped and defined more completely through Kafka than any other writer, and certainly through him rather than any Czech literary work, though one such latter would seem especially predestined to portray the city. This fact is probably one of the involuntary reasons why some Czech literati have repeatedly tried to represent Kafka as being a kind of Czech in disguise and thus to extricate him somewhat from German literature by sleight of hand. Among other things, the American practice of determining nationality according to the country of one's birth has been, incidentally, useful in furthering efforts to classify Kafka as a "Czech writer." This is patently absurd, for an author belongs to the spiritual representation of the language in which he thinks and writes. [When Kafka once wrote to his Czech girlfriend Milena Jesenská: "German is my mother-tongue and hence natural to me though Czech is much dearer to my heart"—one must keep in mind that this utterance is not a "literary" statement but one addressed to and fashioned for his Czech sweetheart. Czech doubtless had a "hearty" sound also for Rilke as it does for everyone who knows this language in native terms and who perhaps grew up in a Czech environment (just as Kafka, Rilke, Brod, as well as the author of this book did) or knew how to speak the language.]

Our Prague German, frequently enough maligned and certainly not lacking in accent though free of all dialect, was able to preserve itself pure and unadulterated on that isolated language island of Prague since the middle ages precisely because it was not exposed to the whittling and dialectal affects of the German used in the provinces and in the country. This was a unique blessing for literature, for we Prague Germans wrote and continue to write in the language in which we live and talk day-in and day-out. Yet this was also true of Karl Egon Ebert or of Rainer Maria Rilke or of Egon Erwin Kisch. There was never a chasm between the literary and the common language for the Prague Germans. No inner necessity to shift, regardless of how unconscious it might be, was ever necessary. This complete coincidence of daily speech with that of literature is probably the great and powerful secret of the Prague German writers with respect to form and effect.

In the Prague of Expressionism

It was especially true of Kafka. Anyone hearing him speak also heard him in every line he wrote down to the subtlest nuance. This is the secret of inner identity which we Prague Germans cherished and preserved as long as possible and which is now, of course, disappearing with the last of us.

FK

EDISON AND KAFKA

In Prague there was a coffeehouse called Edison. The owner was Mr. Turnovsky, the father of one of my older fellow students. The American inventor, who was staying in Prague in 1911 and who liked to observe the goings-on on the Wenzelsplatz (*Václavské náměstí*) from a window desk, gave Mr. Turnovsky permission henceforth to call his place Edison. A large photograph of the "Wizard of Menlo Park" hung on the wall above the desk and was adorned with his autograph. I once sat beneath this picture with Kafka. "That document is memorable," said Kafka earnestly but with that soft touch of irony that also attached itself to his most serious utterances. (One had to be careful, for he would, as it were, express irony ironically, not to emphasize it but actually to neutralize it.)

Americans came to Bohemia only rarely at that time. Most of them visited Karlsbad and Marienbad, and a few probably then also came to Prague. Edison's visit had therefore to be particularly impressive. At that time he was already an older man with a genuine American face molded by energy though he also had about him a touch of the artistic, a Promethean something quite suitable to the Bringer of Light, the practical genius with his 1200 patents. Kafka noted in his Diary for 11 November 1911 that Edison had observed "in an American interview following his trip through Bohemia that the relatively higher level of development in Bohemia resulted in his judgment from the heavy emigration of Czechs to America and that the returnees from time to time brought back with them a new kind of striving from yonder." This conclusion was probably correct only to a very limited extent. Its main basis may well have been the fact that one of Edison's best-liked colleagues, the Prague engineer Kolben, returned home from America and very quickly became an industrial leader. However, Kolben was not a Czech but like Kafka a member of the German-Jewish community of Prague. But also hailing from Prague was a Czech student and friend of Edison, the engineer František Křižík, who introduced the arc-light for street lighting purposes in Prague and who also built the first electric streetcar there. My sitting with Kafka beneath the Edison photo was pure coincidence, for Kafka visited coffeehouses only infrequently. But occasionally he did go to the Continental, the Arco, and also the Edison. And I recall one other occasion when Kafka was sitting with a rather large group under the Edison picture following a recital by that amazing German elocutionist Ludwig Hardt, and listening intently for hours to Hardt recounting magnificent stories about Eastern Jewry.

Kafka's diary entry about Edison and his interest in the phenomenon Edison were by no means incidental but were part of that American magnetic field that began to find expression in 1912 in the early sketches of the fragmentary novel *Der Verschollene* (*The Forgotten Man*), subsequently published by Max Brod as *Amerika* (of which the first

chapter "The Stoker" ["Der Heizer"] had
already appeared in 1913 in Kurt Wolff's
series "Der jüngste Tag"). The most important of Kafka's sketches of America in this
novel was his diary entry of 11 September
1912 entitled "Dream." The dreamer, namely
Kafka, experiences himself in the middle of
New York harbor.

> I found myself on a jetty of square-cut
> stones built far out into the sea. Someone, or
> even several people, were with me, but my
> awareness of myself was so strong that I
> hardly knew more about them than that I was
> speaking to them. I can remember only the
> raised knees of someone sitting near me. At
> first I did not really know where I was, only
> when once I accidentally stood up did I see
> on my left and behind me on my right the
> distant, clearly outlined sea with many battle-
> ships lined up in rows and at anchor. On the
> right New York could be seen, we were in
> New York Harbor. The sky was gray, but of
> a constant brightness. I moved back and forth
> in my seat, freely exposed to the air on all
> sides, in order to be able to see everything.
> In the direction of New York my glance
> slanted downward a little, in the direction of
> the sea it slanted upward. I now noticed the
> water rise up near us in high waves on which
> was borne a great cosmopolitan traffic. I can
> remember only that instead of the rafts we
> have, there were long timbers lashed together
> into gigantic bundles the cut ends of which

kept popping out of the water during the
voyage, higher or lower, according to the
height of the waves, and at the same time
kept turning end-over-end in the water. I sat
down, drew up my feet, quivered with pleasure,
virtually dug myself into the ground in delight, and said: Really, this is even more interesting than the traffic on a Paris boulevard.

This dream vision is the experiential parallel to the turbulent harbor of the entrance
to New York in "The Stoker," to which vivid
personal reports by visitors to America and
certainly also the description of the arrival
in New York in the "American Notes" of
Charles Dickens contributed. Kafka also
hoped, to be sure, that his book would be
read like a Dickens novel, "only enriched by
the more brilliant lights I borrowed from the
times as well as the less brilliant ones that I
myself imposed." The most important addition was, of course, Kafka's "visionary precision," fired especially by the "prodigious
foreign traffic" which is described with so
much gusto in "The Stoker." His imaginings
were so precise, that in *The Forgotten Man* he
projects American freeways, which he had
never really seen, in a powerful and completely fitting picture, thus: "A powerful light,
continuously being refracted by the multitude
of objects, disappearing and diligently re-

appearing, and which seems so corporeal to the distorted eye, as though any minute a pane of glass covering everything would come crashing down violently over this freeway." Gigantic masses of accumulated energies, natural as well as technological, are released in that metaphor, and anyone knowing American highways will corroborate the genuineness of this intense vision.

Kafka's description of the traffic throngs of New York is no less objective. It seems as though he had just now studied the metropolis carefully, fifty years later. "Streets, in which people in great and undisguised fear of being late rushed madly and thrust themselves forward in cars running at full speed . . . . gigantic cars, so striking in build and so brief in appearance, that one had no time even to notice the presence of passengers . . . . columns of cars, five abreast and covering the width of the street, drove bumper-to-bumper, so that no one could have crossed the street . . . . at certain locations, when realignments became necessary because of the pressures of heavy influxes of cars from the side streets, the entire flow of traffic was stopped and then gradually began to move on again slowly bumper-to-bumper. . . . However, at times the traffic did fly by only to quiet down again as though controlled by a single brake."

Still another concrete picture: "The bridge connecting New York with Brooklyn hung neatly over the East River, and it trembled when one squinted. It seemed (from a bird's eye view) to be entirely void of traffic and below it lay the smooth band of water." The psychological pregnancy of this picture corresponds to the clear view of sociological phenomena, so that Kafka, for example, is able to portray in fact the situation of an American elevator operator very impressively and indeed even more accurately than, let us say, Theodore Dreiser, who of course wrote on the basis of actual observation and as an American. However, when Kafka in the opening lines of "The Stoker" has the Statue of Liberty swinging a sword instead of the actual torch, he was by no means guilty of a lapse of the pen or of his vision. He was intent upon looking back of the scene much as Hawthorne had done (in his introduction to *The Scarlet Letter*) in observing the heraldic American eagle above the custom house of his hometown Salem.

Allusions to America already appear in Kafka's first book *Meditation* (*Betrachtung,* 1912): for instance, that dream wish in a single pregnant sentence "to become an Indian" (possibly related to the diary entry about battles between Indians and American federal

28

troops), or the reply of a pretty girl to an admirer: "You are not a broad shouldered American with the build of an Indian, the steady eyes, and a skin tinged with the smell of green lawns and the waters flowing through them; you have not travelled to the great seas and on them. And so please tell me, why I, a pretty girl, should go with you." Ironically intended? Of course. But at the same time also seriously and sadly surveying himself. In addition also a reproach of the kind an admirer of today would have to expect from many a pretty girl. Kafka's diaries contain observations about the girls of New York, young, professionally active, and beautifully dressed; about the life of a department store attendant in Chicago and the general situation there; about the Czech immigrants in Nebraska, the American elections and the American party system (based on a lecture Kafka heard by the Czech social democratic politician Soukop); about somebody who wanted to know "why Americans feel so well even though they curse with every second word." The personality of Benjamin Franklin preoccupied Kafka to an extraordinary degree, especially psychologically. From Kafka's "Letter to My Father" (November, 1919) it is apparent that Kafka gave his father a copy of Franklin's autobiography to read, so as to draw his father's attention to the reciprocal relations between Franklin and his father. (Something of Franklin's clearsighted albeit affectionate realism is also reflected in the story *Eleven Sons.*

Kafka's interest in America, his store of information as well as his intuitive artist's knowledge about the land across the sea (comparable in many ways to Goethe's, who also could accurately describe Boston harbor and from inner experience knew more about America than books and personal reports could have provided) are not at all the direct cause of the consuming interest of Americans in Kafka, whose name is used and abused as a literary household expression as often as Freud's is as a psychological one, or that of Einstein as that of a sworn witness "that everything is relative." Indeed, one can today regard the preoccupation with Kafka as a universal phenomenon (which is also acquiring prominence in the countries beyond the Iron Curtain, even in Kafka's homeland), though Kafka's impact really reverberates most strongly in the Anglo-American sphere. I was astonished already in 1939 when I encountered the phrase "Kafka-like" in a run-of-the-mill daily report in the London *Daily Telegraph,* that is, an obvious use of a name which presupposed a common understanding among average readers. However, in America from

1941 on I have regularly and cumulatively
come upon Kafka's name and that not only
among authors and intellectuals. The name
had become a general designation for the psychological problems of the individual within
certain groups troubled by all kinds of inse-
curities and by unattainable or inadequately
comprehended religiosity. They were convinced that they recognized themselves and
their frustrations in Kafka's characters, that
Kafka's own personality was problematical,
that his autobiographical works are powerfully refracted over the reader like the magic
light hovering over the American highway,
thus driving introverted people to a high level
of identification. In this process they overlook
the integrity of Kafka's realism, his humor,
and the magnificent irony by means of which
he rose above the phenomena, thus preserving
for them the very character of the problem
(as Goethe once suggested), and his penetrating eye which laid bare the unfunny primal
character of things and of human beings.

People interpret Kafka's actuality as proof
of a fusion of his visions (of anguished frustrations within a cosmic bureaucracy) with
certain painful manifestations of the day
which are by no means limited to specific
areas. His true greatness lies in the validity
of his images. Every metaphor always in-

cludes more than its creator intended inasmuch as every image enjoys an autonomous existence and, if it be genuine and precise, develops meanings which at the time of its origin lacked any objective correlatives. Thus, today a Goethe might be incapable of assessing the currently prevailing profundities of his symbols. Today they suggest a world he could not possibly have imagined. Their greatness lies in this continuing power of interpretation. The materials of which symbols are made can find release, when they are problematical or based on time-space conditions, and then attain to new relationships. Consequently, Brod's interpretations of Kafka have as much validity in their way as do those, for example, of Wilhelm Emrich about two generations later.

The later readers of Kafka may well and without serious loss overlook some of the significant stimuli of his pictures. Those who were acquainted with Kafka and his environment knew, of course, that the guard (in *Before the Law*) was a direct play on the bearded, grim looking, heavily cloaked doormen with pointed hats who stood watch with goldheaded pikes at the great doors of the palaces of Prague aristocrats from whose inner recesses an indelibly bright splendor shown forth which the doormen would not

Memorial Plaque at Kafka's Birthplace. (Photo, courtesy, Prof. Johannes Urzidil; photographer: František Blízek)

Kafka's Grave in the Straschnitz (*Strašnice*) Cemetery, Prague. (Photo, courtesy, Prof. Johannes Urzidil.)

even permit us boys to glance at from the
sides. The significance of the dialog between
the doorman and the man from the country
requesting admission is many-faceted and has
undergone variations. Kafka's pictures are actually not pictures but the reality behind pictures wherein the universe and existence become manifest. Existence is after all only
symbolic, for the tragedy of the symbol lies
in its incessant and futile seeking after what
is being symbolized. Thus, America precisely
with all its realism which Kafka sought to
capture and give form to was for him a symbol. But the incessant seeking for the content
of the symbol is also the pervading anxiety
which can be confronted only with irony. "My
essence is anxiety," Kafka writes in a letter
to Milena. Nor does this anxiety disappear
before the gates of Paradise. Indeed, it is
precisely there one hears its loudest shriek-
ing. The contemporary American rightly
senses in Kafka's insight into the soul structure of the individual the most pertinent social criticism of the age. *The Forgotten Man,*
properly entitled *Amerika* and though fundamentally different with respect to problematic
areas from the continuation of the line of
development of (Goethe's) *Wilhelm Meister's
Journeyings,* is placed in the very midst of
a world caught up in the most realistic and,

sociologically speaking, the most profound
decisions. As a consequence, Kafka's actuality became so enormous and it is therefore re-
warding to keep in mind the apparent antith-
esis Edison-Kafka, for Edison, as formerly
also Franklin, represented the American
dream-wish. Despite great admiration one
never experiences either in Proust or Joyce
the *tua res agitur,* the personal anxiety, as
intensely as in Kafka. Consequently, the
American reader has a direct feeling of being
addressed by Kafka, because behind all of his
questions there rises ominously the great
problem of freedom which we thought had
already been answered. That problem is, however, basically a religious one and only superficially political. The possession of mechan-
ical apparatus for lifting the world off the
horns of its dilemma cannot deny the true
substance or meaning of *The Penal Colony.*
In the desperate effort to determine when to
apply the fateful lever, one suddenly becomes
aware that one is sitting on it.

Karl Rossmann, hero of "The Stoker" and
of the novel of *The Forgotten Man,* the latter
of which necessarily remained a fragment because Kafka had planned a happy ending for
it, derives from the period when my physics
professor shouted down to me angrily from
his podium: "People like you we formerly
sent to America." I got there, to be sure, a

little later and for reasons other than those regarded as essential by my physics teacher. However, I also re-encountered Kafka there, alive, venerated, looked upon as the spirit of the age but also rejected with scepticism. The actuality of the American skyscraper afforded all sorts of endlessly interrelated Kafka-like corridors. Angel Flores's (editor of *The Kafka Problem*) five- and six-year olds ran toward me in the hall of their home shouting "Kafka, Kafka" like an Indian battlecry resounding from the endless grass stretches of the prairies, and waiting in the living room were three American authors each of whom was engaged in writing a book about Kafka and whose wives had with them the exact division of Kafka's day in Prague. My wife observed that she "once had a rendezvous with Kafka at three in the afternoon at the *Pulverturm* (*Prašná brána*)." "Impossible!" interrupted a very young American woman, "he kept office hours till four o'clock in the Workers Insurance Co." The teenagers were that well informed about Kafka twenty years ago already. However, Gertrude Urzidil still insisted that he had met her at three, thus indicating that one should, according to Goethe, not be so precise about positive things. One should rise above all that ironically and thereby maintain for it the character of the problematical.

FK

THE REALM OF THE
UNATTAINABLE

Kafka's short prose piece *The Next Village* seems in the first instance an autobiographical statement. Kafka knew his grandfather and noted a remark of the latter, a statement common to all grandfathers throughout the world, to wit, "Life is short." Because his grandfather, like all men, had imagined or hoped that his life would be longer than it now seemed, he qualified his remark by adding that the brevity of life was "astonishing." "Life is astonishingly brief." Obviously only a grandfather could afford adequate temporal assumptions for such a perception. It seems that thus far Kafka has presented us with the picture of a comfortable family situation but at variance with the one actually prevailing in his own home. He required only a single sentence to establish this simple situation. The comfortable nature of the situation gets itself expressed by the iterative. "My grandfather was wont to say." In other words, one listened frequently to Grandpa's utterances.

But now there follows that which transmutes the foregoing into a parable, a very colorful allegory, which reminds us of the following:

The eightieth aphorism of Lao-tse reads:

> A small country with few inhabitants where, though there be tools which can do the work of ten or a hundred men, (the people) may be induced not to use them!
>
> Where the people may be induced to regard death gravely and not to move to distant places!
>
> Where, though there be boats and carts, there would be nothing to load them with and where, though there be cuirasses and arms, there would be nowhere to drill in them!
>
> Where the people may be induced to revert to the use of knotted cords, to savour their own food, to admire their own clothing, to take their ease in their own homes and to delight in their own customs!

> Where, though a neighbouring country may
> be within sight, so that they hear each other's
> cocks crowing and dogs barking, yet the in-
> habitants, till they die of old age, would never
> meet one another! *

What is the decisive premise for the nature-
related Golden Age which the Chinese sage
regards as the ideal? First of all, the limitation to a minimal member of criteria, for example, that it is unnecessary to fan out abroad,
and that it is even proper in the case of extreme longevity not to aspire even to the next
village, though it might be so near that the
crowing of the cocks and the barking of the
dogs there disturb the inhabitants of the neigh-
boring village. Ovid in describing his "aurea
aetas" emphasized the absence of the desire
to travel as a virtue (*Nullaque mortales
praeter sua litora norant*). And Thoreau
assures us that he knows the world thoroughly,
for he had travelled around in Concord many
years.

We should note at once that Kafka himself
never accepted the pose of renunciation and
resignation. His was the passion of seeking
and of flight, the two forms of virulent desiring, whereas resignation and renunciation are
rather grandfatherly. The meditation of the

* From Lao-tzŭ, *Tao Te Ching, the Book of the Way and
its Virtue*, trans. J. J. L. Duyvendiak (London: John Murray, 1954).

grandfather, however, merely signifies that his astonishingly short (actually astonishingly long) life acquires in recollection a remarkable compression. So much has happened in this life that there is almost no place for it within the space of recall, indeed so much "that I can for example scarcely comprehend how a young person could come to the conclusion to ride to the next village. . . ." Note the phrase "for example," suggesting that there might be additional support for his point of view, or also of course "for example I can scarcely comprehend," that is, I comprehend it in part but not completely (one of Kafka's cautions when presenting a point of view); or, I comprehend it only "scarcely as an example," that is, I present this example of my grandfather's inadequate comprehension and ask: How can a young person decide to ride into the next village? (More clearly: How is it at all possible for a young person to decide even only to ride into the next village) without the fear that—entirely aside from unfortunate accidents (after all, how can he reach a decision without fear, indeed, how can he even exist without fear?)—obviously the time span of an ordinary happy life (if there is such a thing, of course, though happiness is mentioned here only as general local color of the customary as opposed to unfortunate aberrances) is simply not long enough by far for such a ride.

Not even a lifetime extending to grandfatherliness would begin to suffice, because the remoteness is actually so immeasurably great and the time so immeasurably short that one would probably have to expire during such a ride before reaching one's destination, however near it might seem. Kafka as well as his grandfather do not at all insist that the remoteness is really so great and the time actually so short; they say merely that the space-time projection must necessarily be a component of the fear of such a young person. The point of this prose piece is not the compression of reality or even the elimination of the time concept, nor of the brevity of life per se or in retrospect, nor space projections of geographic nearness or remoteness, but solely and alone fear. What Grandpa, who is no longer engaged in doing but only in reflecting, believes that he can scarcely comprehend, is the fearlessness and brashness of the young person, his uninhibited ability to decide. The sum and substance of the parable, which presents dogma and demand, lies in the concept of responsibility and can be illustrated by a statement of Goethe: "The person who acts is conscienceless; only the reflecting person has conscience."

The parable is a tremendous consternation, astonishment that there really are people— probably even most people—who without fear, reservation, or conscience dare to make a decision and carry it out, people to whom it never occurs to keep in mind the far-reaching ramifications and consequences of their decision and its realization, acting accordingly therefore outside of morality and getting by without it; indeed, life conceived of as happening actually is realized without reflection, indeed it must be so realized, for it can in general only have color and be called life when reflection is absent. It is amazing and regrettable that Kafka becomes aware of himself outside this viable truth. Goethe observed in his *Maxims and Reflections:* "There is nothing more dreadful to behold than boundless activity without a basis." Note, please, the concepts "dreadful" and "boundless." "Boundless activity" also seemed disturbing to Lao-tse. People who want to be happy ought to undertake as little activity as possible, for they are not equal to the responsibilities. To revert to Thoreau: Even the deepest thirst for knowledge can be satisfied within the smallest space. Concord suffices for learning to know the world and even knowing it thoroughly. Tolstoy, an acknowledged spiritual relative of Thoreau, has the idea resound in his masterful narrative "How Much Ground Does a Man Require?" Here in connection with Kafka one needs also to conjure up Kierkegaard, who developed his religiosity from the elements of fear and responsibility. These are, of course, biblical elements. The fear of things and people, of the mundane phenomena, the fear of self find their release in the fear of God, which is regarded as the essence of wisdom; and the avoidance of evil is that understandable responsibility with which man from the beginning is enfeoffed by God but which he skips over in the fall from grace by means of his unreflecting activity.

The style of the parabolic part of the grandfather's statement is the characteristic Kafka-like interminable sentence containing parenthetic digressions and seeming never to want to end. Like life itself which it comprehends, this sentence is labyrinthine and at the same time lucid, abstract yet concrete, a realistic determination without pathos. It is full of reservations and elaborations just like the world itself ("that I for example scarcely comprehend"—"without fearing"—"entirely apart from"—"already the period of the customary happy course of life"—"by far too inadequate"). The sentence about the next village reveals itself even more clearly than the story about the doorkeeper as being the

uniquely legitimate form with biblical under-
pinning of the amalgam of the mundane and
the transcendent.

Fear (or anxiety) are for Kafka religious
consequences and as such generate thought
and provide form, not—as *angustiae* suggests
—a throttling bottleneck of physiologically
conditioned anxiety and not the fearfulness of
the philistine, of which Goethe clearly wanted
no part (not of fear itself without which life
is impossible, but rather of the fear of the
philistines, who fear that which would never
be fearful to the thoughtful or pious person).
Even the scream in Kafka's diary: "Fear of
night, fear of non-night" (18 October 1917)
is not physiological but rather a religious
emotion (day as non-night; night being the
actuality). When he characterizes his own
being as anxiety (in a letter to Milena, but
also recurrently elsewhere in his letters and
diaries), we are reminded of the god-produc-
ing *timor* of Statius, of a condition of productive fear, for "no one sings so purely as those
in deepest hell; what we regard as the song of
angels is their song" (to Milena). This kind
of religiously conditioned, productive anxiety is present in the building of *The Great
Wall of China* or in the endless and life-long
migrations of *The Giant Mole* (*Der Riesen-
maulwurf*), in which the allegorical as well

43

as the actual animal seeks to protect itself against unforeseeable threats. This same kind of anxiety persists also in the superbureaucratic labyrinths of life by means of which the castle holds off the villagers and the surveyor, man restrains man with the help of institutions and courts in *The Trial,* and the immeasurable and incalculable utopia wards off the immigrant in the Rossmann novel. But the while fear produces gods, songs, architectures, and institutions, it is permanently subject to the consciously responsible impugnment of the reflecting conscience.

The problem is, however, the following (and that is for Kafka as well as Kierkegaard man's most basic conflict), namely, that man does not penetrate through the walls of conscious responsibility to a decision, let alone an act, but seems rather to have had these imposed upon him and even required of him by life for life's own sake. If you can't reach a decision, you are passing up life. That is sin, for life is a religious obligation. If you do make a decision, however, then the avenue of responsibilities opening up before you is so endlessly long, that you will never realize your decision. And thereby you become sinful. On the other hand, should you act without having made a responsible decision, you are equally sinful despite the fact that certain dialectically well-undergirded ideologies respect action beyond the limitation of conscience and also of sin. Man is man only by virtue of facing up to man's problems, which result from the activitation of his awareness of responsibility. The conflict cannot be resolved for us, however, in Far Eastern fashion by avoiding the ride into the next village, for the Golden Age antecedent to the problems is gone, assuming that it even ever existed. Grandpa can scarcely comprehend how a young person can decide to ride into the next village although he himself as a young man probably did so or at least observed others doing so. He himself (or the others) may perhaps never have "decided"; they just rode off without letting conscientious scruples arise. If so, someone might ask, so what? The answer: So everything! For every deed does not become sinful only in the light of its consequences; it is already sinful if it occurs without complete reflection about its implications (even when the act seems harmless), Grandpa sits there as though unable to understand life despite having lived it. And that is completely correct in and of itself, because there is an unnegotiable chasm between life and comprehension, and the world is a crease that never unfolds.

The parable *Before the Law* is conceptually

the essence of Kafka's moral existence whereas structurally it represents the nucleus of his artistic being. "A doorkeeper stands before the law." The law is represented as a building in front of which, that is, before its portals, a porter, a doorkeeper, is standing. His job is obvious. Anyone wishing access is subject to his scrutiny and shall not get past him. This at least is the customary significance of doorkeepers.

The law as a building is an authentic image. "In my Father's house are many mansions" says the gospel. The law represents the truth living within which can be the special privilege of certain persons. (Flaubert: "Ces sont dans le vrai" is repeatedly cited by Kafka.) The obvious meaning is not, of course, the "law" codified by men from certain phenomena, but that law which determines human existence, the "moral law" by virtue of which man has his moral being and is thus man and which like the starry heaven arouses awe and amazement. The law in Kafka's mind's eye is, however, much more than the Kantian law and certainly also much more than all of juridical systems he may have come to know while he was studying law at the German University in Prague. His ideological house of the law is built essentially according to the specifications of the Jewish

46

corpus iuris, comprised of the Thora, that is, the precepts, and their clarification in the Talmud. It is not simply that Kafka has in mind Jewish law as such; he chooses it merely because it is for him the most immediate basic illustration for which anyone could substitute his own morally binding legal code. Kafka envisions the noble construct of a being reassured and comforted by means of divine regulation and liberated from curse and persecution.

The guard standing watch before this house of the law is consequently not a Jewish *shammash,* a sexton, but rather some kind of trusted person controlling admissions, whose exterior unavoidably suggests a middle-Asian Mongolian area of origin. That contrary to all of the foregoing, however, Kafka proceeds from Jewish images becomes immediately apparent in his second sentence. "A man from the country comes to this gate guard requesting permission to enter into the building of the law." Why specifically a man from the country? For years I have pointed out that Kafka is using a talmudic term here, common in Hebraic usage as *am ha-arez* and meaning roughly "country folk" or "untutored layman" in contrast to a consecrated man of learning. (The Greeks would have said "a Boeotian.") This *am ha-arez* or man from the

country has a consuming wish to be permitted
to enter into the law, so as to live within it
like all men or at least most men. He does
not want to be an outsider but rather like all
the others. But the doorman does not want
him to enter now. The word "now" is important. It suggests a possibility to the *am ha-
arez*. He will probably be granted permission
to enter later. "It is possible," says the doorman, "but not just now."

The door to the law stands open, as indeed
it always must, but the doorman must surely
be a giant because he blocks out the whole
view, and it is only when he steps aside a
little (and seemingly coincidentally), that the
man from the country can look in a bit though
even then he has to stoop a mite. All this requires some effort, however, and has no relation to the man himself. Everything depends
upon the arbitrariness of the doorman, that is
to say, if the *am ha-arez* happens to be just
able to cast a casual and quite superficial
glance across the threshold of the law. But
the effort as well as the distorted posture of
the man requesting admission only make the
doorman laugh with derision. "If you find it
so irresistible, then just try to get in despite
my refusal. However, please note that I am
powerful. And I am only one of the lesser
doormen. But there are other doormen from

room to room, one more powerful than the other. Even I can't stand the sight of the third one anymore." A whole series of rigorous tests are envisioned before the candidate may be permitted to graduate into the actual realm of the law. (One is almost reminded of Freemasonry or *The Magic Flute*.) The basic question remains, however, as to whether he is really a candidate?

But we are convinced that we can immediately spot Kafka's suspicion. The unknowing person longing for the obviously self-evident, for the application of an (apparently) universal right, for example, to enter into the law might become aware of the inclination to deal independently and heedlessly with the grim doorman, who has confronted him as being conscience and the mentor of responsibility and has now commenced to frighten him. Beware of what you are letting yourself in for! I already am inconquerable but I am only the beginning. Once you have entered then things will become progressively more disturbing and threatening for you. It is expressly so stated: "Such difficulties the man from the country had not anticipated." It will seem to him that somewhere, somehow things are not going right. Why should admission to the law be so dreadfully hard? The man from the country hesitates a bit and considers, whether he ought not just simply enter. But the sight of the doorman is so frightening, that the *am ha-arez* desists and concludes rather to wait for permission. Note that he decides not to decide.

The frightfulness of the doorman is revealed particularly by his foreignness which is described (fur coat, pointed nose, long, thin, black Tartar beard). Heine's verses "To Edom" come to mind. Despite all that the doorman does not appear to be wicked. He even provides the man from the country with a chair so that he may sit down sideward from the door to await permission there to enter into the law. Thus the minions of the law even offer us certain conveniences but really only for the purpose of extending endlessly and gruesomely the difficulties they create for us. (Synthesis of informal forthrightness, as cultivated mendaciously by the German popular magazine *Die Gartenlaube*, and sadism the reverse thereof.) For the man from the country continues to sit on the proffered chair for days and years repeating his efforts to be admitted. His pleas exhaust the doorman who subjects him anew to repeated interrogations in which many pointless questions are raised, for the doorman has no intention whatever—something the man from the country simply does not know or refuses to admit—to admit him on the basis of his responses to questions. The doorman just is not there—but the man from the country does not know that either—for the purpose of really preventing admission, should the waiting man give up waiting and simply walk in. However, the man from the country does not so decide, he desires and insists upon specific permission. Thus he comes upon the idea of bribing the doorman with his goods. The sadistic doorman submits but also interprets his conduct with the tolerant words: "I accept only to prevent you from believing that you have neglected something." The doorman is that concerned about the welfare of his victim. Related matters may also be found in *The Trial* and *The Castle*. "Our offices accept bribes to simplify matters and avoid unnecessary discussions, but we achieve nothing thereby." A man may pray but he does this on his own responsibility. (*This*, because the prayer approximates a repressed rebellion against the approved course. It remains questionable at the very least, whether the higher powers are moved by the prayer. Boards, eternal or temporal, act just as the "Circumlocution Office" of Kafka-like Dickens does. "In order to have an appointment you have got to have an appointment. But you haven't got an appointment, so you can't get an ap-

pointment." And Thoreau emphatically repeated the biblical sentence: "Ye are not
under the law, but under grace" (Rom. 6:14).
However, grace must be taken by the forelock.

The man from the country grows old and
grumpy waiting for grace of this kind. His
difficulties seem not of his own making but
solely of the stubborn doorman, whom he has
been studying for years even to the extent of
becoming acquainted with the fleas in the
doorman's fur collar. In the undignified and
childish way of an old man he now even begs
the fleas to urge the doorman to grant admission. He has lost all dignity and self-respect.
His eyes have dimmed. The only remaining
thing he can recognize is the brilliant glory
emanating inextinguishably from the law. It
is the glory of sojourn, of comforting residence, of existence "dans le vrai," the solemnity of the *schechina*, the presence of God
among men, the glory of His Splendor lighting up the prayer of the community. The
man from the country discovers a reflection
of this glory unattainable by him.

Now just before his death, however (and
Kafka reports that all experiences of his age
were gathering in his mind just as Grandpa's
whole life was compressed in recall), just
before his death, already weak and faint, incapable of lifting up his stiff body, he gathers

his strength for a final question and signals
the doorman to bend his ear. But the doorman was disinclined. His orders were after
all, as we know, not to guard the door but
only to let the man from the country get on,
if he so decides. "Well what do you still want
to know?" he asks unpleasantly. "You are
insatiable." And now the *am ha-arez* poses
his fateful question, which he was completely
incapable of asking earlier, for it is a question implying years of maturation and the
bitterness of despair: "All men, of course,
strive to attain the law. Why is it that throughout the years no one but myself has requested
admission?" And as the doorman realizes that
the man is approaching the end, he shouts at
him—he has to shout in order to still reach
the already deafening ear: "No one else could
gain access here because this entrance was
reserved just for you. I am going now to close
it."

This finale corresponds to that of *A Country Doctor*. "Cheated! Cheated! Once you
have followed the false alarm of the night-
bell, there is no returning." Everyone has a
door to the law, to existence "dans le vrai";
if he neglects or gambles his entrance away,
no recovery is even possible. The man from
the country—and everybody is such a man
from the country—is irrevocably stuck, for

entrance into the law should of course occur by means of following the law although it could be achieved only by disregarding the watchman, for after all the watchman serves only as a decoy. Cheated! Cheated! The blame devolves upon God, who ultimately within himself becomes obligated to redeem. *Before the Law* is paradigmatic of the totality of Kafka's theological work, this unfinished (because it cannot be completed) argument with God, which finds comfort only during the exceptional hours of armistice in the password: "Writing as a form of prayer." The prayer accomplishes a change of venue for the debate. (The *regula* of St. Benedict reads: *Laborare est orare*.) But prayer is also always an accomplishment for the world, and only the praying poets deserve their name. The greatest of them surely pray even though this is not always apparent.

Before the Law is permeated with that realistic humor which Kafka brought to bear in a burlesque and scurrilous way precisely on serious contexts. If in a world of uncertainties, obstacles, and incessant preparations there were also unimportant non-essentials, then this very world would be divisible and somewhat comprehensible, so that a proper course of conduct and action could be found. However, there are no unimportant non-essentials. Precautions must consequently not neglect even what might seem insignificant. We must even take seriously whatever seems casual, including of course the most ordinary. However, all phenomena occur in variable proportions whereby they become unusual, deformed, grotesque but also, be it said, ever new and interesting, so that one may, indeed should, speak conveniently about the most customary thing as though it had never existed. In the last analysis nothing exists except miracles (a statement of Kafka). Consequently Kafka devotes a scientific scrupulosity to every detail—even to the fleas in the fur collar of the doorman—which—and Kafka knows this—when imposed onto the background of a gigantic soul problem, appears as irony.

This irony is the tart fruit of compassion for the creature, whose individual peculiarity irony exposes to an ever new and insoluble tragedy. The insoluble is a challenge to satire. Inasmuch as everyone is peculiar, he cannot really relate to some model. He would gain access to the law only through his very own door. That he fails to recognize this simple fact and instead deals endlessly with a monstrous doorman, reveals a curious disparity. The parable bridging the unknown void between the divine and mundane worlds makes

use of the abstruse (also on occasion in the
gospels).

Much of Kafka's prose continues the
anecdotal-aphoristic line of development followed by Claudius, Lichtenberg, Hebel, and
Heinrich von Kleist, all of them authors whom
Kafka venerated highly. The anecdote and
the aphorism, the latter of which corruscates
particularly brilliantly in his diaries, were
a shield against the fragmentariness to which
he fell victim irrevocably in the novels. This
judgment is not to be taken formally as if
Kafka were unable to sustain the long dura-
tion of the novel or because his relatively
early death prevented completions, but rather
that complex problems and genuine conflicts
can be resolved more readily by aphoristic
formulation than by narrative. Though the
definition of a novel remains moot, it is nevertheless true that its extended form finds expression in resolution and equilibrium attain-
able only in complete conformity with nature, that powerful tranquilizer of all circumstance. Hence, a brief look at Kafka's
relation to nature might be productive.

Antiquity, living in unbroken relation to
nature, did indeed leave us many torsos but
few fragments. Conversely, about the middle
of the second Christian millennium a gradual
advent occurred of skeptical reservation, of

the will to know and of knowledge (including "the inability, for example, scarcely to comprehend"), and immediately that epoch of incipient occidental experimentation became one of significant fragmentariness which coincides in essential features (for example, in the case of Michelangelo) with an unreconciled relationship to nature. Michelangelo—like Kafka, later—is completely anthropocentric.

As a man Kafka was surely a friend of nature. However, in his writings and diaries viable nature is rarely mentioned (most frequent allusions occur in the so-called *Oktavheften* of his literary remains). In the fragmentary novel called *Amerika* one finds landscapes, to be sure, but they are, to borrow a phrase of Goethe, constructed by the "precise imagination" of Kafka (and are consequently surprisingly apropos). In the other writings nature appears only fragmentarily, in dream elements or abstractly, in the form of unnamed flowers of a metaphysical kind, or as anthropomorphic animals with symbolic meaning. (In the 700 pages of diary covering fourteen years nature or landscape occur scarcely ten times and then only incidentally.) In Kafka's letters to his beloved friend Milena Jesenská one does read about green bouquets, sprouting birds, towering mountains, brilliant sun, and wide heavens, about lively landscapes full of insects, lizards, and birds. The reason for all this is, of course, that his fascinating Czech girl-friend stepped into Kafka's life like a natural phenomenon herself.

In antiquity the relation to nature was one of involuntary belonging, so that an identity resulted also between artist and work of art of the kind which tolerated no fragment. Kafka successfully attained this kind of absolute identity in anecdotal and aphoristic statements, in which he accordingly had great confidence and therefore lent himself to their creation. The anecdotal and aphoristic is, of course, the obvious carrier of humor as well as satire (a fact clearly demonstrated by Lichtenberg, Claudius, Hebel, Kleist and others). The exaggeration or blowup of a detail, the miniature reproduction of a gigantic phenomenon, the absurdly large shadow a pigmy casts depending upon his posture in the sun, the spectroscopic view of rapid occurrences, contrasts, and connections of this kind reveal the comic latent in and affecting all things, even the most solemn, most profound and even also the most tragic things insofar as they are of this world. Kafka's satire captures the nonsense, the confusion and the unattainable, something painfully contradictory by nature, which he then investigates pitilessly with a sadistic precision as in *The Penal Colony* or as in the case of Poe in *The Pit and the Pendulum*. On occasion painful matters are projected in a way so bizarre as to occasion no regret whatever. In moments like that Kafka becomes the perfect raconteur, an artist who knows how to transmute a phenomenon into the absolute all the while reserving the discrepancies of its relative existence for laughter.

In the anecdote *A Daily Confusion*, Kafka reports with patronizing dryness on an everyday occurrence which results in daily confusion. However, in so doing he demonstrates precisely the unusual character of the pedestrian situation. His target is the miraculous aspect of everyday. All education desires to lay bare the causes and effects of things but thereby diminishes the ability to be astonished. Men hope to make the world knowledgeable by disenchantment and orderly by reduction to the commonplace. However, man loses every genuine relationship to phenomena by that process: He does not respect miracles because they are uncomfortable, disturbing, and therefore indecent. (Weaklings admit to no enthusiasm, never appear surprised and knew everything better long ago.) We are back again in the area of religion, for the reduction of life's miracle to the commonplace is related to the loss of faith and religion. But Kafka sees nothing but miracles. The following aphorism expresses the horror of reducing the unusual to the commonplace: "Leopards break into the Temple and drink up the contents of the sacrificial vases; this keeps recurring; finally one can calculate it in advance and then it becomes a part of the ritual." It is not the recurring of the event that makes for reducing it to the commonplace but rather the advance calculation to which educated people seek to reduce everything, but everything.

However, the descriptively applied word "commonplace" has a special satirical meaning in the anecdote. Just look at what you regard as commonplace! Mr. A and Mr. B are engaged in a sober business deal. Both gentlemen default on their appointment. Nothing could be more ordinary. But what caused them to default? The extraordinary circumstance that on the day of the appointment A requires ten hours to reach his rendezvous with B whereas he would ordinarily have needed only ten minutes. In the meantime B has gone to meet A. We are not told why A required ten hours instead of the usual ten minutes to keep his appointment with B, but we can explain it ourselves. A would like to conclude the business deal with the mercantile side of himself but something or the other within creates an unconscious resistance which delays his progress despite his incredible rush to get there. Things get so bad that he hurries past his presumed partner standing in the door of his own house and tells him, the very man with whom he wanted to close a deal, that he has no time for him because he has to run off to conclude his deal with him. Even worse: Hearing upon his return that his part-ner was already waiting for him upstairs, he rushes to meet him so hard that he stumbles and acquires a painful sprain which prevents him from getting to B, who in the meantime rushed angrily down the stairs (probably past the injured man) and finally disappeared.

Kafka was well acquainted with Freud's theory of failure and even better acquainted with Goethe as the most decisive proclaimer of the significance of the unconscious, but needed neither of them for his depth-psycho-logical realization, for precisely the reactions issuing forth from the unconscious constitute the pith and substance of his most character-istic satire. Actually, however, his concern in *A Daily Confusion* was for its ethical aspect rather than its psychological or satirical as-pects. The confusion people suffer derives from the fact that most people (hence "every-day" confusion) do things or desire to do things their innermost conscience resists. Consequently either they never get to the point of action—and that would be the better alternative though also the more painful one—or their action goes awry in some unnatural, dishonest, unethical manner. The creature appears as a sacrifice to the nature superimposed on it in its desperate attacks on an apparently inconquerable determinism. Businessman A defeats his own purpose because of his unconscious conscience. The beautiful and terrible rider from Bamberg (reference is to the famous equestrian statue in the Bamberg Cathedral) does not change his mind because of the next village. However, between the two was Hamlet. ("Thus conscience doth make cowards of us all.")

Kafka's realism also actualizes (and does so in long-run terms) the spatially and mythically remote. The distant penal colony, the African Arab oasis, the China of the parables, the America not only of the great novel fragment but also of many other isolated aphoristic pieces and of the "dream journeys" (*Traumfährten*) in the diaries (may Hermann Hesse forgive me using his coinage), and in particular also the utilization of the antique myth, all of this indicates enduring inclinations and compulsions but always on an objective basis. At times, however, the objective correlative requires corrections.

Whereas the man from the country vainly wastes away his life before the entrance to the law, *An Imperial Message* paraphrases the destiny of vanity and of the unattainable by inverse means, namely, by proceeding from the innermost recesses of the law toward the person waiting. The power of this allegory becomes all the greater, of course, because it takes place in an eastern world of the gradual and timeless, a world in which Kafka's intuition felt at home.

It is not as if man cannot realize salvation on his own and under clearly impossible conditions, but that salvation itself—the imperial message—simply can't reach him. Salvation is purposed, the messenger is curtly dismissed, he exerts himself to the utmost to deliver his message but he just can't find his way out even through the innermost rooms of the palace. (We are reminded of the many doormen stationed before the halls of the law.) But even if the imperial messenger did fight his way through the innermost chambers, nothing would have been accomplished. In that event he would have had to fight his way down the stairs, and even if he succeeded in doing that, nothing would have been gained.

The courtyards would have to be crossed, and then the second surrounding palace, more courtyards and steps, and still another palace, and so on through millennia. But even if finally he did push through the outer door, the residential city would only lie ahead. Nobody gets through here and especially not with the message of a dead man. The very message containing salvation is bound to the entire misery of the infinite. Salvation is promised to us. It hurries toward us. We ourselves, if we are worth our salt, move toward it. But infinity lies between, an imaginative idea obviously permissible only in parables. However, man is not allowed to digress from his intention to be prepared for salvation despite the absurdity of the vanity of it all and the almost complete improbability of salvation. He must conform to that paltry word "almost," for his salvation, if there really is such a thing, depends upon it.

Kafka's work reports on the inescapable machinery of life; of its bureaucratic mechanization which holds a man for interrogation incessantly, and makes accusations against him whose substance and purpose are never really known to the accused; compels him to admit crimes he never committed; subjects him to incomprehensible and refined tortures and punishments. It would be absurd, how-

Teingasse (*Týnská ulice*), Old Inner City, Prague. (Photo, courtesy, Prof. Johannes Urzidil.)

Old Roman Gate, Charles Bridge, Prague. (Photo, courtesy, The Bettmann Archive, New York.)

ever, to undertake to interpret Kafka's work from any political aspect. He sought only to record the irrevocable dilemma, the irresolvable conflict, and the contradiction within the individual who gets lost in the labyrinth of his own internal and external institutions. With the inviolable zeal of the prophets, Kafka is, however, not lacking in grace and is continuously filled with pity for the grotesque contortions to which all creatures are subject. The will to unconditional truth, which alone can bring about the correctness of the metaphors, makes enormous demands on the writer. "It is hard to speak the truth, for there is only a single truth, but that truth is viable and consequently wears a changing living face." (To Milena.) Kafka was aware that every definitive statement carries within it the symptoms of contradiction and of deadly disintegration for the responsible person. Consequently, as literary artist he always faced up to the question: At what point does anyone have the right to summon people to consider his own insights? That is no mere literary problem but rather a religious one.

Swedenborg once said: "Conscience is the immanence of God in man." The daemon of Socrates, the "Deus in nobis" of Ovid (*agitante calescimus eo*) is the carrier of conscience, which alone makes possible the genuine deed but also brings about the misdirection of substantial and important undertakings, puts the brakes even on the decision to ride to the next village and delays the entrance into the law. When Kafka called his first book *Meditation*, his first great decision in the area of intellectual endeavor, he definitely chose the side of conscience mindful that he was thereby renouncing action, that he would continuously have to wait for the imperial message, which probably would almost never come—for no one gets through here—but for which man should nevertheless always hold himself in preparedness, for— as he already told himself in 1912 in his diary: "Even if salvation fails to come, I want to be worthy of it every minute."

FK

ASSOCIATION WITH SIRENS

Kafka's anecdote *The Silence of the Sirens* is as puzzling and fascinating as the mythical singers themselves who never get a hearing in the story. People have been trying in vain since the beginning of time to ascertain the extent to which reality played a part in the background of the original myth. The effort was unproductive, of course, because the myth was presumably the actual reality from the beginning. Materialistic pundits have identified the famous mischiefmakers alter-

nately with oriental owls or penguins, others
have viewed them as obtrusive mountain shep-
herdesses who sang enticingly in the service
of cannibalistic bullies. More imaginative interpretations accepted materialized sunbeams
or planetary effects, and the series was extended so as to include mermaids, nymphs,
and demi-fish-women. Some dreamy-eyed sail-
ors insisted, they had observed high-bosomed
mermaids who seductively sang soprano col-
oraturas to them; their more clear-eyed companions, however, maintained that their bud-
dies had actually seen only sea-cows who
were neighing in shrill high-pitched tones.
In all this and disregarding the exchange of
the elements one thing remained certain,
namely, the feminine character. The birds
with human heads as seen by Odysseus or the
water nymphs encountered by Henry Hudson
and Captain John Smith on their ocean journeys to America, all of them invariably
showed up female characteristics just like
the undine, melusine, and loreley images of
a similar order. The most feminine propensity
they shared in common was their absolute inability to tolerate disillusionment. Most of
them also availed themselves of the most feminine means of enticement, namely, the song,
if we disregard that siren reported by Nor-
man Douglas, the most ingenious of siren ex-

perts, to have been captured at the beginning of the fifteenth century in the Zyder Zee and to have enjoyed a long pedestrian life thereafter in Haarlem without speaking a word. One might possibly relate this silent siren to Kafka's extraordinary mutes.

A clear genealogy of the three female magicians of antiquity, Porthenope, Ligea, and Leucosia, has been handed down to us, indicating they were descended from Phorcys and Keto. Phorcys, a very sinister fellow, was also the father of the Graeae, of the Gorgones, and of the dragon Ladon who stood guard over the apples of the Hesperides. Originally, the sirens were easily the most beautiful of this gruesome clan. But because they failed to stand by their playmate Persephone when she was kidnapped from Hades, Demeter magically transmuted them into pinniforms. From then on they beset innocent travellers out of vengeance for their fate and to this end settled down for practical purposes on the cliffs of Capri. In any case they are located there in the Homeric cosmography just as the Amalfian side of the Cape of Minerva is made to serve as the dwelling of Circe. Gregorovius and later also Douglas seem to suggest that they had personally encountered the sirens in that area without having suffered any injury from them. In Goethe's precise imagination they are made to occur with great exactitude on the shores of the upper Peneus and in the rocky bays of the Aegaean; however, that was before they migrated to the Capri area as a probable consequence of the various westward journeys of the Hellenes. [On the return from Sicily Goethe's ship might almost have been wrecked solely because of the undercurrents around the Isle of the Sirens (*Italian Journey*, 14 May 1787). One of Goethe's drawings (presumably for the second part of *Faust*) depicts sirens singing and playing the flute on the cliffs. Goethe's library contained the *Basic Mythological Dictionary* of M. Benjamin Hederich, in which the sirens are depicted as "notorious whores, who attracted the passersby to them and then undressed them."] We are told that the Argonauts rode past the sirens unmolested only because Jason and his very famous companions happened just to be listening to the song of their fellow passenger Orpheus. The sirens could not compete with him anymore than they were able to evade defeat in their duel with the Muses, who plucked them clean as punishment. Their feathers nonetheless grew back in again.

At all events Odysseus was the last to see the sirens as feathered creatures and because they failed to impress him they threw them-

selves into the sea in a typically feminine reaction. We have three remaining versions of
their subsequent destiny. According to Eu-
ripides they continued living on in Hades
with Persephone. The second version has them
swimming about in the oceans as demi-fish.
The third insists that they transformed themselves into the cliffs of Capri. This latter version appears to be the most probable one and
the one coinciding best with the original myth.
For something sirenlike and wondrous had to
be hovering over the ozone of Capri, thus
corroborating the circumstance that Mr. Wre-
ford, a British publicist of the nineteenth
century, visited the island just to spend an
afternoon but remained there more than thirty
years till his death. Later similar incidents
happened there repeatedly just as they are
said to occur in Hawaii.

All details such as the foregoing require
mention if one wishes to interpret Kafka's
siren story properly. One needs especially to
recall the Homeric version. It occurs in the
twelfth song of the *Odyssey*. One must take
care not to forget that Odysseus himself is
the narrator, and that he was notorious as a
teller of tall tales, who wanted to appear even
more important in the eyes of the lovely
Nausicaa than he already was in fact. Thus
he reports that Circe had warned him of the

sirens who at that time were sitting not in a
group of three but as a couple on a flowery
meadow, surrounded by bones, decaying human corpses, and dried-out hides. In this macabre setting the gruesome ladies bewitched
all who came near their dwelling. No one
who listens to them will ever again greet his
family at home. It becomes evident here how
well Circe knew her Odysseus who preferred
his homeland even to immortality. *Ithacam ut
videret, immortalitem scribitur repudiasse*
(Cicero, *De legibus* II, and Dion Chrysostho-
mus, *Orat.*, XIII). And it is also Circe, of
course, who suggests that the ears of his companions to be stuffed with wax and Odysseus
himself to be bound to the mast, lest he despite all warnings still desire to hear the sirens
(a curiosity on the part of Odysseus rightly
anticipated by Circe on the basis of her own
experience).

The journey of Odysseus then transpires
from the Cape of Minerva, where Circe resides (palace ruins continue to be pointed out
to visitors), westward, presumably to get—
despite all nostalgia for home—between the
Pillars of Hercules to fabulous Atlantis, a
journey which Dante later recreated by divi-
nation and also almost allowed the Ithacan
to complete. But the latter himself tells the
Phaeacians how the wind suddenly subsided,

the water became smooth, and the calm sea
began to sparkle. Symptoms indicating the
proximity of the sirens. Wax is quickly stuffed
into the companions' ears and Odysseus has
himself bound to the mast (note please: with
ears open). And immediately he hears the
song of the sirens, which sounds immeasurably seductive in Greek, enticing already in the
first hexameter with seventeen full vowels
(and only fifteen consonants): *Deur ag ion
polyain Odysseu mega kudos Achaion:*
"Come, famed Odysseus, great pride of the
Achaeans," thus did the bird-women warble,
"come, and you will journey on pleased and
wiser than before" (*pleiona eidos*), "for we
know everything about Troy and the destiny
of the Argives, and in general about everything happening on earth" (*Idmen d'hossa
genetai epi xthoni poulyboteire*).

Flatteries of this kind would surely be appropriate even to outsmart the tied-up hero,
particularly inasmuch as no trivial, mundane
tomfoolery is being promised here, but instead wisdom, though the sirens were obviously fibbing and promising Odysseus more
than they could ever have delivered. The latter, more fortunate than Adam, was not being
exposed additionally to the coaxing of a
woman but could rely completely on his fellow mariners, who according to instructions

would only bind him more firmly to the mast, so that the whole expedition would be able to escape the Phorcyadic call-girls.

Thus far Homer or rather Odysseus. Something vastly different transpires with the myth in the hands of Kafka. He had discovered that Odysseus had himself riveted to the mast and also had his ears stuffed in order to feel absolutely secure against the feathery fays according to the old saw "doubly sewed holds more securely." Kafka's Odysseus is entirely Kafka's own. A mere rearrangement would not satisfy him. The sirens, too, are Kafka's sirens, for they have at their disposal not only the weapon of song, but an even more terrible weapon, namely silence. And according to Kafka's version the powerful prima donnas would not have sung as the ship of Odysseus approached. Indeed, the Ithacan believed they were actually singing but that their song could not reach him because he was doubly secure. In reality they did remain silent however. Now this kind of silence might suggest that the persistence of Odysseus not to permit himself to be seduced under any circumstances straightway deprived these females of the power of speech. But Kafka attributed to them the power to remain silent as a conscious weapon.

He thus inverts the traditional myth (just

as his New York statue of liberty at the opening of his *Amerika* novel extends her greet-
ings not with a lofted torch but with a drawn
sword). The precautionary tricks of Odysseus
are successful obviously only at the expense
of his heroic reputation. By pushing the interpretation a mite farther, one would expect
the sirens to have remained silent because
they knew they could not be heard anyway,
and so their silence would have disgraced the
cunning man before the gods as well as before
men. Kafka appends still another conjecture
according to which Odysseus still overtrumps
the silence of the sirens inasmuch as he knew
about it but acted, this overwise fellow, as
though he assumed they were singing and thus
held out to the gods "the apparent event only
as a shield of sorts."

Kafka paraphrases the theme of *anxiety*
and shifts the myth in the direction of human
weakness. Odysseus is not a bad choice for
such a shift. He is the opposite of the stupid
Achaean daredevils, he is a hero *malgré lui*.
Plato relates in the *Politeia* that Odysseus in
Hades desired nothing more in the event of
his rebirth than "the life of a simple private
man." All this recalls Kafka's wish projection
of a life *dans le vrai*, of the life of the "common man with regular habits." He could have
filled volumes with his complicated descrip-

tions of that man. Anxiety must, of course, be sharply distinguished from cowardice. It is possible to interpret anxiety, which incessantly probes the possibilities of a disaster in all its facets, also as being a ritual for preventing the disaster. If this ceremonial of anxiety were neglected, then life would be taken too lightly and the door opened to misfortune.

The anecdote about the sirens parallels Kafka's leopard aphorism. The aphorism describes the abolition and trivialization of the uncommon behavior of the leopards, who with human calculatedness suck the sacrificial vessels of the temple dry with a regularity that threatens to become a ritual. The leopards are subsumed into the daily ceremony even though the reduction of the ceremony to the absurd is also meanwhile dependent upon the unpredictable arbitrariness of the leopards. For it is possible that the leopards might one day fail to show up just as the sirens reduced Odysseus' calculations to the absurd by confronting him with their plan whereas he was convinced that he had taken care of them with his own plan. Furthermore, the plan of the sirens has to misfire because it is simply impossible for Odysseus to become aware of it, or if he does so, then he had long before subsumed it within his own plan.

After all, a parable has its beginning in the infinite and eventually winds up there.

One might be inclined to think that even the most meaningful parody of antique materials and motifs is derived partly from the high-schooler's compulsion to make a monkey of his Greek teacher. Is it he to whom Kafka in his gloss *Poseidon* wants to show the lord of the sea for what he really is, namely, the calculating business manager who has been charged with the regulation of the waters? Charged, for he fullfills a task because he has to and like most officials takes little pleasure in his work but keeps busy by virtue of the law of inertia. Outside the sphere of his business he is sick to his stomach and within it he has no prospects, for at best he might anticipate becoming the administrator for his own recreation of a private lake and that would be in essence really a demotion. And so despite his vast influence he is unhappy, even a little derisive, and is annoyed with the distorted pathetic images people project of him, whereas actually he loses himself in idle calculations with the result that he never got a clear view of the seas whose accounts he keeps, much like the president of a gigantic wood products concern who never took a walk in a real woods. Poseidon's sole hope is the end of the world. Only then, shortly before the end, after reviewing his final calculation, might he perhaps allow himself a little trip around his oceans. In a fragmentary story Kafka describes an official, taken from daily life, who is the very counterpart of his projection of Poseidon, namely, an "accountant spread across his ledger like a frog, a shortsighted, somber man, quiet, moving up and down slowly and solely in response to his weak breathing." Poseidon is also shortsighted; he never saw his seas; he lies spread out above his ledger sad and grieved; not like a god of the universal waters, but like a frog of the swamps. The pantheon of antiquity was subject to the same frustrations and unattainables as the mundane world except that the result among men is tragic whereas among the gods its serves as parody. For the Olympians must be especially careful regarding their pathetic superiority since it can so easily become risible (indeed, it has become so in many literary projections since Homer).

Poseidon would have only a single means of salvation from frustration and the unattainable, namely, total destruction, which however could represent no escape because precisely that is destroyed which was supposed to be saved. Poseidon's observation that he would learn to know his seas shortly before the destruction of the world is consequently and clearly labelled by Kafka as incredible frivolity. It is apparent that Poseidon will never get to know his oceans although he will continue to administer them, whereby in so doing his divine immortality represents only a special kind of added punishment. Were Poseidon mortal, death could be helpful to him. Instead he must experience an anthropomorphic displeasure but without ever ridding himself of his immortality. Among men the fear of death counterpoises the fear of immortality.

The transmutations of myths, that is, their propagation, is a legitimate function of the literary artist; indeed doing so is his real profession. He stands above historical sequences and geographic juxtapositions leaving the anachronisms to time and the anatopisms to space. Thus, Schiller could without any concern anachronistically utilize the lightning conductor in *Wallenstein,* Goethe could adduce weeklies and death certificates in *Faust,* Wagner was able to introduce lilacs into *The Meistersinger,* and Shakespeare could locate Bohemia on the sea in *The Winter's Tale.* Motifs are symbols independent of time and space; Helena remains young and beautiful regardless of her age; and a

good theatrical play remains so regardless
of its costumes. The myth of the sirens lives
on through ages and the moods of men in a
hundred variant forms, attaches itself to the
stela over the grave of Sophocles, whose sirens
represented soul-birds as well as the convincing character of his art, or speaks and
sings forth from Goethe's dripping river maid
in "Der Fischer" and even resounds in contemporary ears in the form of the warning
and howling sirens of factories, police-cars,
ambulances, and airraid alarms. All such
things disguise danger but also serve as enticement, for the simple reason that everything profoundly fearsome—even the fear-
someness of death—always contains within
itself a variant of demoniacal enticement.
For we play with death from the time of our
childhood and up and into foreign ministries
and ministries of war. Propagandists of all
shadings dote on the actual or imaginary
heap of bones the while warbling sweet promises, and so one must not only have oneself
bound to the mast but also—as with Kafka—
have both ears stuffed, so as to resist the
pleaders. Wherever propaganda finds no open
ears, it loses its reason for being, for whoever cannot hear can also not feel—or so
people believe.

The complete silence of the sirens would

not be a demonstrably and really effective weapon until and unless it were perceived as such, namely, if the sirens had gazed silently into the face of a listening and unbound Odysseus. This he probably would have been least able to resist. Consequently—according to Kafka's projection—he paid no heed to only an imaginary song. As for the sirens, they probably remained silent neither from stubbornness nor from embarrassment because they lacked a compelling theme, but simply because they had good reasons for assuming that fear of an imaginary song was much more powerful than that of their actual song. In any case, they destroyed themselves by their silence and their destiny of that day was completely sealed as it relates to Odysseus. But because mankind has an insatiable need for sirens, they live on in other forms. Indeed, no one can be sure of the extent to which he himself is not continuing their mythical functioning.

FK

BRAND

Some insist that Brand never lived, that I invented him as a pseudonym for my own early literary efforts. Nonsensical conjectures of this kind are based on an erroneous report in a literary almanac in which the name "Brand" appeared as my pseudonym. I have, however, never published any creative writing under a disguise except when I was a senior in high school at a time when high schoolers in Austria were prohibited from publishing. Even then I did occasionally publish some poems in the Sunday Supplement of the *Prager Tagblatt* under the name of "Hans Elmar," which seemed romantic to me and which I had adopted from some long forgotten epic (F. W. Weber's *Dreizehnlinden*). Obviously, all of my fellow students knew who Hans Elmar was. I took care of that in a youthful desire for fame. But one of my classmates, Hans Gerke, much more talented than I, not only eliminated me from the field but put me to shame by boldly publishing his poems under his own name in the aforementioned paper. His triumph reached its peak when one of his poems was violently attacked by none other than the famous Karl Kraus of Vienna in the latter's *Die Fackel*. I had to wait almost another twenty years for a comparable success. In the interim following Gerke's display of virtue I too used only my real name.

There was, however, something to the assumption by some people that Brand never existed inasmuch as the name was not documented in any of the Prague church registers, birth records, or other official documents. However, "Karl Brand" was indeed a pseudonym albeit not mine but that of another young contemporary by the name of Karl Müller. I learned to know him shortly before our graduation and later on we met fre-

quently in the famous Café Arco together
with the other Prague authors and writers.
More about this and the developing friendship between Müller alias "Brand" and me
may be found in the story *A Young Man's
Legacy,* which is one of the panels of my
book *Prague Triptychon* (*Prager Triptychon*)
and which has been frequently reprinted elsewhere. This panel is actually an autobiographical report containing actual historical
details yet structured in the form of a narrative. In any case, I tried to reconstruct
with extreme accuracy the living atmosphere
in which Brand moved and the manner in
which he reacted and expressed himself. Werfel's 1931 story *Kleine Verhältnisse* (*Small
Relationships*) may be regarded as a counter-
piece. Werfel describes the milieu of a poor
family corresponding to the prototype of the
(Brand) Müller family situation. I referred
to this fact in my epilog to the Werfel story
published as a textbook by S. Fischer in 1955.

Werfel had been casually acquainted with
Brand since 1913. To call this relationship
a "friendship" would be pathetic. The fact
that Brand, a Christian, was in the truest
sense of the word of proletarian (and not
petit bourgeois) origin whereas the older
Werfel was the son of a wealthy Jewish
family would not at all in and of itself have

prevented the development of such a friendship. As regards Werfel the relationship developed from the very beginning as a result
of his strong and ever present feeling of
commiseration, pity, and human compassion
whereas for Brand the basis was his un-
bounded admiration for the affirmation of
life and the confident assurance of the genius.
Brand was consumptive despite a double
pneumothorax operation. His best medication
was his lyric-epic talent and sharing the company of his literary acquaintances. He died
in 1918. Werfel and I visited him during
his last days and I stood by at his deathbed
in the ancient and poor courtyard apartment
of the dismal Baroque house on the Radetzky
(later the Kleinseitener) Platz (now Malostranské náměstí), a deteriorated building in
whose complex storeys, macabre corridors,
recessed loges encircling the courtyard, and
dead-end attics one could get lost like one
of Kafka's accused victims.

While Brand was still ambulatory—till
about the beginning of 1918—I often took
walks with him and saw him home usually
from the Café Arco through the inner city
and past the ornamented Charles Bridge. He
knew that he would soon die and spoke of it
in his last days with more curiosity than fear.
He made me promise to publish his literary

remains. He was convinced that to be published meant perpetuation. *Non littera scripta sed littera impressa manet.* I lived up to that promise to the best of my ability. In 1920 I published an anthology of Brand's poems and prose pieces entitled *Karl Brand, Das Vermächtnis eines Jünglings (The Testament of a Youth)* [Eduard Strache: Vienna-Prague-Leipzig]. I asked Werfel, already then living in Vienna, to write an introduction and I myself added a little epilog to the book. Brand was, indeed, to appear arm in arm with his comrades. Werfel even copied off his introduction in his own hand and in beautiful calligraphy from his draft and I still retain this holograph today in New York.

Brand's literary productions, which I already knew from hearing him read them, were never great or world-shaking works of art but everything he wrote revealed the cotyledonary germinations of a significant literary artist whose destiny, whose mortal illness would deny him ultimate fulfillment. Above and beyond this Brand symbolized a youthfulness distracted by the search for new forms and a pure ethos, and this youthful striving made him lovable. Considerations of this kind color Werfel's prologue (distending but also compressing temporal events) as well as my epilog. According to Werfel "the power of the generation entering upon life under the ill-fated star of these events [viz., the war, and its psychological and social assumptions] was the avowal of shipwreck, the compulsive and unconditional leap into the sea." I could evaluate Brand a little more positively. A definite artistic type seemed to me becoming articulate through him, "once at least with full solemnity," but I was also convinced that I was beholding individual treasures even amidst his creative unwieldiness. Gustav Janouch in his book *Conversations with Kafka* alludes to a brief discussion about Brand which probably took place some time in the fall of 1921. Janouch was eighteen at the time. In the conversation he mentioned my publication of Brand's literary remains which had appeared just shortly before and he reports what Kafka allegedly told him about the deceased: "He was such an unfortunate young fellow who got lost among the centenarian Jews of the coffeehouses and died. And what else could he have done? The coffeehouses are today Jewish catacombs. Without light or love. Not everyone can stand that." The "centenarian Jews" of the Café Arco are obviously intended to be parabolic. Kafka was physically a kind of elder at the coffeehouse table at which he sat with Brand on occasion though he himself was only thirty

to thirty-five at that time (1913–1918). What
he had in mind, of course, was the metaphysical age, the hundreds and thousands of trou-
bles burdening the Jewish diaspora all over
the world. The coffeehouses could well be
the catacombs wherein they could pursue their
rites in relative security. Accordingly young
Brand appeared to Kafka to be a misguided
stranger, destined for death, among the patriarchs of the coffeehouses. Kafka himself
was neither a regular nor frequent visitor in
the coffeehouses. But when he did go, he imposed on the group, even when he spoke but
little, a definite coloration suggesting that he
was there regularly, an impression which in
fact was in a certain spiritual sense completely true.

That Brand—in Kafka's view—might have
had the feeling while sitting at the Arco table
that he had got into a labyrinth was correct
in a certain sense inasmuch as Brand-Müller,
a product of the naive milieu of his family
in whose home pious lamps burned day and
night beneath a crucifix and the Madonna,
strayed into a sphere wherein the best minds
were regularly preoccupied with their own
very personal religiosity, though this was infrequently articulated, the while an entourage
of gossipy, know-it-all intellectuals loudly
proclaimed their sharply agnostic-nihilistic

prejudices. Meanwhile Brand was gradually dying and one noticed that he was aware of the fact; and that Kafka suspected something similar in his own case was an open secret, a fact—as I shall show—that would become clearly apparent from an observation by Kafka about Brand.

How Brand got to writing poetry, however, cannot be explained anymore than it can in the case of other literary artists. His home, if it can be called so, did of course share the "poetry of poverty," for which the poor man himself has as little awareness as does the miner for the natural beauty of an avalanche. There are poverty stricken poets, regardless of whether they are good or bad, and rich ones also are sometimes bad or good. And it is easy to conclude that it was probably this "great brilliance from within" (already perceived by Rilke, a metaphor which superficial critics held against him) that ignited the poetic in Brand. A greater likelihood is that the inevitability of death from mortal illness contributed a compulsive power, the literal burning up of the youth, "flame am I for sure" in Nietzsche's words. The intensity of Kafka's creativity in the years he became certain of his own early death, or at least of its probability, is comparable. However, healthy, vital people, filled with the breath of life and assured of longevity, also write poetry, some of it good, and some bad. Silent despair as well as jubilant confidence, both of these can produce their poets, bad ones and good ones alike.

This difference must, however, be kept in mind: Kafka wanted his literary legacy destroyed whereas Brand passionately desired his to be published. In the first instance this distinction is one of superiority. Kafka was great. Substantial portions of his work had already appeared. Though he did not enjoy the far-reaching publicity already indicating the universal fame of Werfel, he was secure in the unreserved admiration or the shy adoration of his friends. He was humble and not lacking in that Flaubertian anguish of doubting his creative powers; but he would have to have been a fool not to recognize his eminence. Because he did recognize his station, he was able to render that well known letter of disposal to his friend Max Brod which the latter fortunately disregarded and thereby preserved Kafka's literary legacy for the world. Next to nothing of Brand's work ever saw the light of day (excepting those few poems I personally got published earlier in the literary review *Der Mensch* of which I myself was the editor, and in a slender memorial volume *Die Dichtung* published by my

friend Wolf Przygode in Berlin). And who
among young poets has not been mesmerized
by the thought that getting oneself published
is the greatest good fortune that can befall
the children of men? There cannot be self-
confidence in a young literary artist unless
he gets this kind of irremissible assurance.
And what poet or writer or artist is completely
free of the necessity for a certain exhibition-
ism? He wants not only to form, structure,
express, represent, proclaim, teach and effect,
but he also wants to put himself on display
in his moments of bliss and despair, both
those things he regards as his most glorious
triumphs and even those he feels to be his
deepest degradations. As a dying man Brand
wanted assurance that not only would he go
on living in his poems, but that he would
actually by means of them be enabled just
to commence to live. I felt the intensity of
his desire anew even after thirty-seven years
when I wrote the story *A Young Man's Legacy*
and thereby reincarnated Brand within myself and once again stood watch at his deathbed.

At the end of this story there is a com-
munication from Kafka to me, which is rea-
sonably well known and is included in Max
Brod's edition of Kafka's letters. In New
York, where I live, these thoughts of Kafka,

embalmed in his own fine handwriting, daily catch my eye together with other lines he indicted to Gertrude Thieberger long before I married her. That statement of his (17 February 1922) picks up the anthology of Brand I had published. These words of Kafka have a special importance, for they are as relevant to the poet Kafka as to his human relationship with Brand, a relationship much more profound than one might surmise after his remark to Janouch. Kafka analyzes the book in a single sentence, culminating on several levels, a sentence which is a classic example of Kafka's ability to completely comprehend a phenomenon in all of its facets and simultaneously to plumb fully its profundities. "First of all, Werfel's quite simple and dreadful truth. . . . , then the death of this young fellow, the screams lasting three days and three nights though actually not a single sound of them was heard and if they had been, one would have walked on a couple of doors further, there is no other 'way out' except this one, and finally your manly and comforting epilog, which one would naturally like best to concur in, if it were not for the fact, common to the nature of comforting, that it comes too late, after the execution." What a sentence! The whole phenomenon Kafka is contained therein. We hear the intonation of his voice. The words acknowledging receipt of the book involuntarily acquire the full weight of a prose piece resulting not merely from the point of view, nor from the immanent power of the style, but rather from the depths of the felt experience, from the emoting of the heart, from an inner anxiety, and from the incipient accusation of self. He calls death "execution."

And all of his deaths stand before us, especially the one in *The Metamorphosis,* a fact, particularly emphasized by two other sentences of Kafka, one of them preceding, the other following his central statement about Brand. They are: "The book reminded me in its essence but also in its structure of *Ivan Ilyich!*" And then: "It is no different with *Ivan Ilyich,* except that it becomes even clearer in *The Legacy,* because every step personifies itself in a particular way." How does Kafka suddenly get to Tolstoy's *The Death of Ivan Ilyich?* I should mention first of all that Kafka had reread this story shortly before writing to me. (Diary entry, December, 1921.) I say "reread" because he obviously had known this possibly greatest novella of Tolstoy for many years. In our literary debates in Prague references to this novella played no little part. I myself read it in 1914, stimulated to do so by the conversations at the Arco table. Kafka must have known it, however, at least since 1912, because his first efforts in connection with *The Metamorphosis* cannot deny the influence of Tolstoy's shocking depiction of the gradual, inevitable, and incomprehensible death of a human being. Now, Kafka's prefigured character Gregor Samsa stood before him as flesh and blood in the person of Brand, who met up with Kafka in 1913 (even to the extent of corresponding accuracies relative to the identical Prague milieu), indeed, Kafka may have seen prefigured in Brand (as in Samsa) his own gradual, inevitable, and incomprehensible death even before the doctors had diagnosed it. And thus the reference to the life and death of Ivan Ilyich in combination with the life and death of Brand may well have been concatenated with the life and death of Gregor Samsa and especially with the life and death of Kafka himself. The cry "Cairo!" which Brand casually but shrilly uttered amidst a painful attack of coughing was the violent breakthrough of a passionate longing for life, a dream-scream for sun, colors, tropical heat, the tantalizing thirst for living of the kind denied to the youth in the grey, mouldy walls of the old Kleinseitener house wherein he passed away. Kafka's passionate love for the opera *Carmen* and its heroine with her con-

centrated vitality was a comparable phenomenon. My wife still has in her possession several written tokens of Kafka, reminiscent of
the time when he took her to performances of
Carmen repeatedly. In 1913 he inscribed for
her into one of the first copies of his first
book *Meditation* a quotation from Mérimée's
Carmen. (See Brod's edition of Kafka's letters.)

Kafka's remark about *The Metamorphosis*
(1916), referred to above, "What have you
to say about the dreadful things going on in
our house?" has a topographic as well as
autobiographic significance. The Kafkas lived
in Prague only a few steps from the Thiebergers. They were next-door neighbors. Go-
ings on in our house? Of course. The person
to whom the dreadful things were happening
was obviously Kafka himself. Almost a year
passed before Kafka's mortal illness was un-
equivocally confirmed by the doctors. But the
truth was, he had earlier already had a confrontation with the deadly diagnosis in *The
Metamorphosis*. He knew there was no salvation for himself but he nonetheless wanted to
be worthy of it every minute. When Brand
died in 1918, when Kafka reread *Ivan Ilyich*
in 1921, and when shortly thereafter he wrote
to me about the Brand book, Brand's fate had
attained for him an ominous prescience.

Tolstoy's *Ivan Ilyich*, Kafka's *Metamorphosis*, and Brand's *Legacy* became intertwined and constitute an entity. Consequently, Brand has greater significance for literature than he himself surmised or than Werfel or I could know in causing his little lyre to resound again posthumously. Perhaps Brand never "lived"—in any strict sense—as a person, never experienced what we call life in any full sense, but he did experience death and there is a kind of death that makes for immortality.

Zeltnergasse (*Celetná ulice*), Old Inner City, Prague. Tein-Kirche to the right. Tower of the City Hall to the left. Hradschin Castle in the background. (Photo, courtesy, Prof. Johannes Urzidil.)

Ledergässchen (*Kožná ulička*), Old Inner City, Prague. (Photo, courtesy, Prof. Johannes Urzidil.)

FK

THE TEACHER OF HEBREW

His name was Friedrich Thieberger, he was
a Ph.D., a student and protégé of the eminent
Prague Germanist Professor August Sauer,
who later also became my teacher. He was
the oldest son of Rabbi Dr. Karl Thieberger of Prague, and though he chose the
profession of high school teacher of modern
languages, his inner vocation remained the
knowledge and interpretation of the sacred
texts of the Jews. Such interpretations were,
however, not restricted to the rational. They

lay instead in the area of his own personal realizations of the scriptures, which he sought thus to interpret in the manner of his own existence. We were engaged in an enthusiastic and youthful argument about the general nature and obligations of religion, an argument which effected deep furrows in our daily lives and even led to mutual rejection for several decades, but later—as is so often the case with good and holy arguments—our quarrels wound up with the most splendid reconciliation. This disagreement afforded my basically Christian being precious insights into the actual profundities of Jewry and of Jewish doctrine, invaluable furtherances, which incidentally also brought me to a better understanding of Kafka than would have been possible in serene reflection, for anyone who never had to struggle with his own religious problems, be he Christian or Jew, can comprehend Kafka only superficially and not basically.

Thieberger and his family were on friendly terms with Kafka, and he once published his recollections of this relationship in a brief study in the German journal *Eckardt*. The salvaging of this forgotten and obscured memoir is important for the closer understanding of Kafka. But above and beyond this, Thieberger (born 1888 in a provincial Bohemian township, educated in Prague, died in Jerusalem in 1958) deserves a special spiritual monument. Already as a young man he wrote verses and theatrical plays and acquired prominence as the translator into German of the poems of the American-Yiddish workers' poet and ghetto-troubadour Morris Rosenfeld (born 1862 in Poland, died 1923 in New York), but these achievements were only preliminaries to the more substantial ones of his later life including the 1936 publication of the standard work entitled *Jüdisches Fest-Jüdischer Brauch* (*Jewish Festivals and Customs*); in addition his book *King Solomon*, published in English in London, which on the basis of new sources affords a description of the cultural and political development of the Holy Land as well as investigations of the three books of the Bible accredited to Solomon; still another English book by Thieberger entitled *The Great Rabbi Loew of Prague* is indispensable to anyone desiring an understanding of the historical Jewish continuity in Prague, hence an integral part of Prague's cultural development, and by that token also indispensable for the interpretation of Kafka and his links to the mystical Jewish background of that city. But whoever desires to understand Kafka merely as a writer existing in arid space and apart from reality, that is, to understand him falsely, must unquestionably first study Thieberger's *Glaubensstufen des Judentums* (*Levels of Jewish Faith*), a brilliant conception reflecting clearly both Jewish doctrine and its realization. In addition to Kafka and his circle of friends Thieberger enjoyed a close and friendly relationship to Martin Buber and to that eminent Jewish historical scholar and researcher of Jesus, Joseph Klausner, whose monumental work *Von Jesus zu Paulus* (*From Jesus to Paul*) he translated from Hebrew into German.

To indulge in ideological quarrels with that kind of superior scholarly mind is both beneficial and sensible. But we also enjoyed friendly discussions and especially often about Kafka, whom Thieberger became acquainted with shortly after his own graduation from the University, in other words, a year or two before I became personally acquainted with Kafka. The Thiebergers at that time lived in a house in the Karpfengasse (Kaprová ulice), the street on which Kafka was born and which later became widely known from a novel of our friend M. Y. Ben Gavriël. That house was situated only a few steps from the Altstädter Ring (Staroměstské náměstí), the Town Hall Square of Old Prague, near and about which the several later dwellings of the Kafkas were located. Thieberger, five years younger than Kafka, regarded Kafka as being "less active than reactive" in conversation. And that observation hits the nail on the head. Kafka never deliberately imposed his ideas upon anyone but rather waited quietly for the other fellow to take the initiative. "But when he reacted in conversation to an idea," Thieberger notes, "one was profoundly surprised, for his words came as though from another world and yet were quite appropriate to what had been said." The relatedness of different worlds, the basic formula of the metaphorical. I experienced this simultaneous being remote and completely present, this superior and at the same time directly involved posture of Kafka again and again and have also written about it. Everyone who came into contact with him had the same experience.

The parabolic essence of the world was always present in him, that twofold and threefold reflection, which of course also plays such an important part in the silent characters of his stories. The unusualness of his presence probably did not quite have the aura of "holiness" but it did have a magnetism which automatically lifted those present or his partner in conversation to a higher level and was perhaps—if you will—"holy" in the sense that no one in Kafka's presence would have dared to utter something "ordinary." An extraordinary phenomenon obviously achieves superiority principally by uplifting the level of its surroundings. It is uplifting rather than condescending. In the Prague of that day we were accustomed to a plenitude of good writers, painters, sculptors, scholars and musicians, German and Czech, Christians and Jews, from labor circles, the bourgeoisie, and the nobility. The breezes of creating and nurturing talent were blowing there. Everywhere it was always possible to admire, enjoy, and discover a multitude of stimuli. But criteria of this kind would not suffice for characterizing Kafka. For it was as Thieberger described it: "When Kafka attended a performance of some kind, there was a hush: Kafka is here! He himself had sneaked in as unobtrusively as possible and would vastly have preferred to flee quickly again from amidst the throng." Quite so! I myself frequently underwent the experience of feeling how the whole atmosphere of a room or a meeting place changed as though by a single stroke. Meanwhile Kafka stood off somewhere in a corner. It seemed, however, as though some unseen attendant had whispered to the lecturer: "Be careful about everything you say from now on. For Kafka has just arrived." This irresistible magic always represented to me evidence of the eternal. And it is still viable today. Never before have I had the definite feeling in the presence of any other genius whom I had the good fortune and honor to meet, of the sudden change in the inner coordinating system of an entire audience or group, indeed even of the actual spatial proportions of an assembly room resulting from the mere silent presence of a personality.

Thieberger made a very lovely observation about Kafka's handwriting apropos of the aforementioned inscription Kafka wrote for Thieberger's sister Trude (later to become my wife) in a copy of his first book *Meditation*. He said, it was "an elegant script in which only the powerful vertical strokes of the great consonants reflected the willfullness of the writer and in which was again recognizable the childlike pleasure he took in the smallest of everyday things as a shield against the shadows of heavy thoughts." It is probable —or so it seems to me at least—that this remark implies a hidden allusion to the prevalence of the Hebrew consonantal alphabet, which is presumably primal and involuntary for every Jew. As regards the "shadows of heavy thoughts," however, I should like to dissent from Thieberger's conclusions only to the extent of observing that I regard Kafka's

childlike happiness in little everyday things
not as a defense. Instead, this joyousness was
an inherent attitude of his toward the world.
(Moreover, Kafka wrote the dedicatory inscription, to which Thieberger alludes, several years before he was aware of the precarious nature of his health; meanwhile
"heavy thoughts," which were always casting
their shadows on him, were in his case anything but egotistically or even physically conditioned.) Interpreters have recognized repeatedly that for him nothing was "little"
and that everything had its autonomous significance for itself as well as for the whole.
One must keep in mind that this was the period of the discovery of and avowed preference for East Asian art and especially also
for the Japanese woodcut in which the virtues of the smallest details were co-equal with
all other values; moreover, Prague—by virtue
of the work of Professor Christian von Ehrenfels and his students—was a source of the
theory of structural qualities (*Gestalt-
Theorie*) which interrelated rather than sum-
marized the origin of the decorative from
out of the reciprocal and reflexive interac-
tions of all of the components, even the most
minute; and finally, the insights of Freud
were just beginning to become widespread at
that time. Hence, in a certain sense, complete-

ness was for Kafka present also in the smallest things, and the little everyday matters
could constitute not only motivation but even
the great materials of literary art. This view
was, so to speak, an idea immanent in Prague
which also became apparent in the case of
Max Brod, of Werfel, and already earlier of
Rilke. Thieberger perceived quite rightly in
Kafka's view the presence of the "love for
the gentle details" (to use his phrase) which
related Kafka to Stifter. These gentle details
were not merely conceived by Kafka as contrasts to something harsh, but rather as a
gentility undergirding the real substance of
things, patience, composure and inner security, and it was such considerations that made
Kafka happy and to which he gave literary
expression over and over again in exotic and
often burlesque contrasts to the general dis-
organization of mankind. (And in this respect he is Homeric.)

Shortly after the First World War Kafka
approached Thieberger with the request that
the latter give him instruction in Hebrew.
Kafka had done a little preliminary studying
in a textbook thereby refreshing his scant
knowledge of Hebrew acquired from religious instruction as a child and as a youth.
Now, Thieberger was pretty well equipped
in Hebrew, as the pious son of a rabbi he

could read and interpret the scriptures and
texts; however, he hesitated at first about giving Kafka instruction, indeed—conscientious
as he was—he rejected Kafka's request because he did not feel that confident about his
ability to converse in Hebrew. "Yet"—so he
reports—"Kafka refuted all of my arguments
with his entreating smile so full of helpless-
ness and excuses for all deficiencies, and so
I finally acquiesced." This sentence reflects
two basic components of Kafka's character.
Namely, the childlike naiveté expressed in an
irresistible, pleading and somewhat helpless
smile, and simultaneously the superior stance
which regarded all deficiencies natural and
self-evident. One could always observe these
two characteristics in Kafka in simultaneity,
not only in his life but also in his writings,
the identity of which with his life is comparable to a similar identity in Thoreau and
Stifter. In describing things or people he almost always approaches them with a naive
petition, he never takes them by storm or by
pressuring, never seizes upon them or upsets
them; but at one and the same time he manifests the superiority of veniality, which, to
be sure, is next-door neighbor to irony.

The instruction in Hebrew took place regularly in Kafka's dwellings at that time on the
Altstädter Ring only a few steps away from

the Thieberger residence. And Kafka, thirty-
five at the time, pursued his studies with the
diligence of a boy thirsting for knowledge
and the conscientiousness characteristic of him
in all matters. "He was very precise," Thieberger said, "about his vocable book and the
written exercises and became indignant upon
discovering any imprecisions in the system of
the textbook." At that time Kafka was certainly already aware for more than a year of
his precarious health, and yet one could not
observe it externally on the tall man of elegant stride, nor was its seriousness appreciated by his friends excepting Max Brod. Consequently Thieberger could not but be surprised when Kafka—excusing himself for
having missed a Hebrew home assignment—
suddenly blurted out: "I am sick, very sick."
Kafka said this in Hebrew. And Thieberger
might well have been frightened for the moment, but he himself was still a young man
and though he had lost his father just a short
while before, his healthy and hopeful nature,
for hope is the chief criterion of health, re-
fused to want to accept the fact of inevitable
illness on the part of another young person.

Kafka's study of Hebrew was not attributable exclusively to a desire to make up a
youthful deficiency occasioned by the inclination of his own as well as countless other

Jewish families toward assimilation; nor was it attributable to Kafka's close association with Zionist friends including also Thieberger; nor was it merely an understandable reaction to the War, which had brought various problems of European Jewry to the fore and tossed them squarely into the middle of the grand confusion of all the other unresolved and probably unresolvable problems of the states, nations, and classes. There is little doubt that the primary reason underlying Kafka's study of Hebrew was his search for a world fundamentally secure and therefore promising for the future, above all else, however—and that should be emphasized—it was the seeking for holiness which European life as well as a substantial part of Jewish life had somehow lost. Kafka certainly did not wish to become a Hebrew scholar. He would have needed a lifetime for that purpose rather than just a few hours of tutoring in Hebrew. He was convinced, however, that by means of some knowledge of Hebrew he would better be able to approach his innermost and central problems, the idea of God and the problem of death, which overshadowed all else and comprehended within itself all questions about the meaning of life, of justice and injustice, of human existence and co-existence. These problems were much too old and profound for even preliminary comprehension by means of a modern practical language or translation whose instrumentation was attuned to much later epochs. It is possible, of course, that texts from the upper stratum of one language, that is to say, of one symbolic system can be interpreted over into the top level of another. Impressive achievements by means of this art are evident in the Bible, in German from Luther to Buber-Rosenzweig. But an intellectual and emotional universe can never adequately repeat itself within the sphere of some other universe of feeling and thought. This fact rather than the mere difference among languages is, of course, the reason for the inability of nations to understand one another, let alone the inability of people sharing the same language to understand each other. For any language is but the essence of a system of stenophonic seals currently in use as a means of mutual understanding within some living and intellectual community. I know Christian theologians who attended and still attend *yeshivas* in Jerusalem for the purpose of instruction at the hands of Jewish biblical scholars in the language of the Torah, the Talmud, and the Cabala, for they had come to realize that they could comprehend and experience their own Christianity only in the language of Jesus and the synoptics.

Thieberger, the rabbi's son and religious scholar, must have seemed to Kafka ideally suited to introduce him by means of the language of the fathers into their intellectual and religious world. For Thieberger himself had not learned Hebrew in the customary way in school but had absorbed and assimilated it from early childhood as an integral part of his maturation for life. And so Kafka received not only instruction in Hebrew from him but religious instruction as well. Perhaps the arguments I was having with Thieberger about religious problems at just the time he was teaching Kafka Hebrew resulted in large part from the very fact that I had structured my Christian Catholic ideology exclusively in German and Latin terms, particularly in the latter, which even today are ready to my hand in any religious context, even more so than the German, so that we—Thieberger and I—were engaged in discussion on different levels and he was certainly a more confident fighter as a result of the traditional security of his life-roots. Consequently, it was a significant and to me unforgettable experience when at the time Thieberger and I, each in his own way, personally encountered Kafka, the

110

former wrote me a long letter detailing his objections to my views but yet according his objections a certain ambiguity by concluding with the words: "Let us relate to each other in the equilibrium of humility," a word incidentally worthy of his close and venerating relationship to Buber. Humility requires, to be sure, not only a basic disposition of the soul but long and profound experience as well. Both of us still needed many years after that time to really draw closer to humility. Contrariwise, Kafka had a great advantage over us as regards humility. That he should even talk to me or occasionally listen to my ideas already constituted humility. Humility is one of the basics of religious existence. Nobody is religious without humility.

Of the conversations between Thieberger and Kafka two seem to me to have special significance. The one relates to Ben Franklin's autobiography which Kafka had read with great interest, as I have already mentioned. Franklin, the inventor, and Edison, the inventor, were obviously characterized by a common, very typical kind of Americanism. In addition, Franklin despite all his realism never denied the religious basis of life. In his daily prayer at evening he turned not so much to God's grace as to God's insight. He petitioned God for "reasonable health," that

111

is, for reasonable well-being, not for unrea-
sonable youthfulness. And so it is precisely
with him that the profound statement, sur-
prising perhaps to an American of today,
originated: "No man has been totally born,
until he is dead." Franklin belonged together
with Rousseau and Goethe to the first great
autobiographical protagonists of the new age
and that, of course, must have moved Kafka
deeply whose total literary output obviously
consisted in Goethe's phrase only of "fragments of a great confession." He writes: "I
am just now reading the life-story of Franklin. My, but there were a lot of children in
his father's house! I wonder how it looked
when all of them sat around the table and
their father at the head of it." Thieberger is
right in observing in this remark a source for
the story *Eleven Sons* (included in the volume
entitled *A Country Doctor*) in which the most
closely related ones are the strangest ones if
only because of their presence. Obviously,
the stimulus derived from the contrast. The
elder Franklin at the table with the multitude
of children in early American family community in old Boston: that was in essence
the image of Kafka's longing, life *dans le
vrai* which he missed so much in the home
of his own father. It was the image of longing on the part of all authors of novels in

which dream castles are sought after whether it be in Goethe's *Wilhelm Meister,* in Adalbert Stifter's *Nachsommer (Indian Summer),* or in the *Grandmother* of the great Czech writer Božena Němcová, much admired by Kafka. Thus are all things related, from Boston to the little Bohemian town of Cěská Skalice, the setting of the *Grandmother.*

Shortly after the death of Friedrich Thieberger's father (1918), Kafka presented the grieving son with a copy of his *A Country Doctor.* The author dedicated this volume to his own father and Thieberger interpreted the gift as being a delicate allusion to the loss he himself had just suffered. In expressing his thanks during a Hebrew lesson he said to Kafka: "How happy you must be to have been able to dedicate your book to your father." Kafka demurred. Obviously he had suddenly come to realize that the dedication suggested a close relationship between himself and his father, a relationship that had never existed, whereas Thieberger had always had a mutually loving relationship to his recently deceased father and always regarded his father as a venerable model. Somewhat frightened Kafka therefore said: "But this dedication to my father was intended as irony. Yesterday I finished a hundred-page letter to my father in which I had it out with

him." Now it was Thieberger's turn to be
frightened. A hundred-page letter! Could one
imagine that there was that much to be settled
between son and father? So the dedication
was intended to be ironical. That it was, but
in two different directions: over and against
the father, and over and against Kafka himself. Its delicate and nuanced mockery im-
plied: "You will, of course, never understand
it" but simultaneously also averred: "I shall,
in truth, never understand you." And so despite its intended irony this dedication seems
to have had something childlike and moving
about it which in turn invalidates at least in
part the complaints and accusations of the
notorious *Letter to His Father.* For a dream-
wish was present at the very moment the
dedication was written, a dream-wish desiring
full recognition as a child and son and simultaneously desiring full comprehension also
of the father, basically a wish that is impossible of fulfillment if one considers that an
unbroken continuity of successive generations
without father-son countercurrents is conceiv-
able only as one of the most extraordinary ex-
ceptions in the development of mankind.

Thieberger was easily the most religious
and unquestionably one of the most orthodox
among Kafka's friends and he of course zeal-
ously observed all of the external prescrip-

tions for Jewish life in the sense of his father.
This was, understandably, a frequent source
of our disagreements. He saw in the external
Mosaic rules of conduct the cultish seal of
the abstract religious ethos which radiates
into the general and into the messianic. I in
turn insisted that all this was no more than a
reflexive adherence to outworn and past matters that had long since lost all religious content. Experience taught me that I was wrong.
For Thieberger, the author of the book about
Jewish customs, a confessional courage was
attached to such adherence, and this courage
of conviction would not tolerate a single vio-
lation—and in addition, as I well know, this
kind of courage stood one in good stead later
on in difficult times. Thieberger thus wore his
spiritual Jewish star long before his—and I
say it with pleasure—and also my friend
Robert Weltsch publicly cried out to his oppressed fellow-Jews in Berlin: "Wear your
Jewish star with pride."

It is self-evident that this kind of attitude
on the part of Thieberger should have its effect on Kafka. Thieberger was also a close
friend of Georg Mordecai Langer and has
written in detail about this important scholar
of the Cabala. Kafka's personal acquaintance
with the Praguer Langer, who for years had
lived among Eastern Jews as an Hasidic and

published his researches in German as well
as in Czech, was brought about by Max Brod.
It was also Langer who continued Kafka's
Hebrew instruction after Thieberger. How-
ever, Kafka directed his chief attention to the
Bible and the Talmud and less to the Cabala
except for its popular and somewhat later
Hasidic forms. (See Max Brod. *Johannes
Reuchlin*, 1965.) Kafka's fellow students
under Langer were Felix Weltsch and the
lyric poet and author of *Märchen*, Miriam
Singer, now living in the famous kibbutz
"Deganja" on the shore of the Sea of Galilee.

Thieberger's religious-philosophical life-
work was infused with the idea of common
Jewish obligation, the motto of which was
kol Israel aréwim sélose, all Israel, all are
witnesses, the one to the other. The significance of this mutual obligation was in Thieberger's view no mere Jewish egotism but lay
instead in its paradigmatic importance for
all the world. And here we sense a reflection
from his friend and teacher Buber: the ancient
and holy concern of the prophets and their
ceaseless messianic purification battle against
the challenges and suffering of existence as
well as co-existence. At this point ecumenism,
which today concerns all of us so deeply and
more than ever before and which relates so
perceptibly to Kafka's intellectual universe,

116

also protrudes into the purview of this discussion. For if for Thieberger on the one
hand the *Book of Job, Ecclesiastes,* and the
challenges of Jeremiah and Isaiah constitute
the basic undergirdings of the Jewish intellectual-spiritual structure, then they also on
the other hand represent a corroboration of
Christian doctrine, so that a recent Pope could
properly proclaim as guidance and warning
to his Catholic Christendom: "We are virtual
Jews!"

Kafka's compulsion to learn Hebrew cannot be attributed to a philological interest,
nor as being merely some kind of Zionistic
concern; it was instead the insatiable urge for
the nearness of God, for the law; for the language of the scriptures is the unique and immediate human element wherein the idea of
God can begin to be experienced. Kafka was
an enthusiastic admirer of the German poet
and writer Johann Peter Hebel. And one of
the stories from Hebel's *Schatzkästlein des
rheinländischen Hausfreunds* (*Treasure Chest
of the Rhineland Friend of the Family*), to
which Kafka's own prose style is so greatly
indebted, he most admired is *Einer Edelfrau
Schlaflose Nacht* (*The Sleepless Night of a
Noblewoman*). The highpoint of this prose
story occurs when the lady begs the forgive-
ness of her maid, sorely oppressed by destiny,

for her sternness when they first met and
promises her help to the maid from then on.
Hebel, who was moved by the purity and
profundity of his own story, makes the comment: "Does it not seem that in the words
of the noble lady one is hearing the blessed
Lord talking in the Prophets or in the Psalms?
A disposition inclined to the good and taking
the part of the miserable ones and lifting up
the fallen ones, such a disposition attracts the
image of God and consequently falls into his
pattern of speech." I happened to be present
at that occasion in Prague when Kafka heard
a reading of this story by the famous German
recitalist Ludwig Hardt and was deeply moved
because the story pays tribute to the language
of the scriptures as being the natural language
of God's nearness and of ethos. All of us were
sitting together later in the Café Edison, including all of Kafka's Prague friends, and
on the following day Kafka presented Hardt
with a copy of Hebel's *Schatzkästlein* inscribed: "For Ludwig Hardt, to please Hebel." This happened some years after the
Hebrew lessons with Thieberger. But all these
little things were closely woven together and
it was necessary to have experienced them to
be able to say: That's exactly the way Kafka
was.

FK

GOLEM MYSTICISM

During the First World War, in 1917, Kafka was for the time being living in a little house in the Alchymistengasse (Zlatá ulička), home of the Renaissance alchemists on Prague's Hradschin just back of the castle above the Hirschgraben (Jelení příkop), which was part of the imperial parks. This highly romantic and ancient corner of Prague, suffused with so much historical atmosphere, was even then a sightseer's delight, albeit there were fewer foreigners in Prague at that time than was the case later on, and during the War there were almost none; generally and foolishly Prague was never regarded as a tourist town. People went to Berlin, to Vienna, and to Budapest, cities included in the Cook's tours, but Prague never seemed important enough to international travel agencies and so went unnoticed, much in the way that rich people from the Moravian Brno or even from the Bohemian provincial towns, except the Czechs proper, regarded it as more *chic* to go to Vienna than to Prague, a dreadful mistake and stupidity which contributed greatly to the later collapse of the Austrian monarchy. Meanwhile all this redounded to the good of the Alchymisten-gasse by keeping it quiet and mysterious. Evenings one could hear the softest crackling and it was an ideal spot for lovers and doubtless also for poets, for nothing about it was artificial or borrowed. The funny little cottages tightly squeezed together, which had served the goldseekers of the melancholy Emperor Rudolph II as workshops and houses, were inhabited by poor folk, who exhibited their miniature establishments to tourists for a minimal fee and on occasion even rented out a small room. During the Renaissance at the time when Tycho Brahe and Kepler lived in Prague as court scientists of Emperor Rudolph II, the mystical laboratories were located in these rooms, in which one sought after the philosopher's stone, synthetic gold, and synthetic man. The famed "Golem" was, however, not created up here on the castle hill in the shadow of St. Vitus's Church, but rather down below in the old Jewish ghetto on the other side of the Moldau river. But it was in one of these little houses in Alchemists' Row that Kafka lived for a short time. He was then working on the stories included in *A Country Doctor*. The time was shortly before his tragic illness had been diagnosed.

The experience of living in Prague on the heights of the Hradschin or in the Kleinseite (Malá Strana) lying below was quite different from that in the Altstadt, the inner city (Staré Město). The Hradschin reflects the royal, the imperial panoramic view, whereas the old inner city shows forth the middle-class and folkish aspects. The differences between the left and right banks of the Moldau were at all times not merely topographic for there were also deep cleavages in deportment and even in speech accents. The Kleinseitner German with its sharp *s* and its short vowels was different from the softer, somewhat cozier German of the inner city. The splendorous palaces of the royal and imperial vassals on the slope of the castle hill give this part of the city its conservative coloration to which the houses of officials and burgers, squeezed in between, were adapted. A little later, in 1878, it happened that the excellent Czech storyteller Jan Neruda captured with fantastic success the quality of life on the left bank in his *Kleinseitener Geschichten* (*Malostranské povídky*), one of the very few creative books about Prague from a Czech pen. Both the Hradschin milieu as well as the Kleinseitner one relate to Kafka. He also had a room there for a short time in the palace of the Counts of Schönborn.

To get from the universe of the alchemists up by the castle to the Jewish universe of the Golem roundabout the Old-New-Synagog of the thirteenth century one had to cross the Moldau by way of the Charles Bridge adorned with the statues of the Catholic saints with which the church triumphant symbolized the victory of its "counter-reformation" over the Protestant (Czech as well as German Bohemian) rebellion of the Thirty Years' War as it also did with the Statue of Mary in the midst of the Altstädter Ring, which statue was torn down in 1918 when the Republic was proclaimed, thus opening up the view toward the bronzed gaze of the religious and national martyr Jan Hus. Kafka lived through his Alstädter Ring days, that center of his exis-

122

tence in Prague, in three stages: First, only near the Pillar of Mary; then in the contradictory company of the Catholic Madonna and the Hus Monument, which literally proclaimed to everyone: *Pravdy každému přejte*, which means roughly: Equal rights for all; ultimately, however, still only with Hus.

But the universe of the Hradschin-alchemists and the rabbinical sphere of the Golem in the Prague ghetto, immediately behind the Altstädter Ring, were bound together not only by the Charles Bridge, they communicated back and forth historically as well as spiritually. No matter what direction Kafka took between the inner city and the Hradschin, up or down, everywhere he found himself completely in the middle of an adventuresome and usually of a half-transmundane atmosphere, all of which one feels in his every written sentence, to a more intense and convincing degree than in the Prague novels of Gustav Meyrink, who with his *Golem* has since 1915 influenced the image of Prague for non-Praguers as well as for many Praguers. The same year, however, marked the appearance of Max Brod's *Tycho Brahe's Road to God*, a substantially more profound novel, much more important from a narrative as well as an historical point of view, and definitely more characteristic of Prague. Meanwhile, however, Meyrink remained for a long time the man of the hour.

It is important to be mindful of the actual and esoteric basis of the Golem myth and the striving of the Renaissance for power over the primal elements and the creation of a synthetic man, to sense the mystery saturated atmosphere in which Kafka developed. First off let it be said that I am not talking about the romantizing hocus-pocus mysticism of Meyrink's novels. Meyrink, whose name reminded Kafka unprettily of a convulsed hedgehog, was himself not a Praguer though he was repeatedly and persistently so designated. He was born in Vienna and his father, so it is recorded, was a minister of Würtemberg and even a baron. In fact, his name was actually not Meyrink; hence Kafka's hedgehog metaphor might be regarded as a classical example of precise imagination. Meyrink had attended school in Prague only for a while and had lived there temporarily. Acidy Walter Fürth called him an "artificial man." His *Golem*, though very famous, was not so much admired by us then as was a greater achievement, his glorious discovery of the *Schöpsoglobin* ("idiotoglobin") whose presence in the human organism was alleged to produce an excessive patriotism, nationalism, and milita-

rism, phenomena which the literary frequent-
ers of the Café Arco have always at all times
regarded as common dangers to existence.
Whatever Meyrink projected in the meantime
about the Prague ghetto, the inhabitants
thereof, cabalistic rabbis, and the Golem himself got widely read, filmed, and dramatized,
not withstanding it was an imprecise recreation of the original Golem saga-cycle. The national and religious essence intermixing and
producing synthetic men in the melting pot
called "Prague" requires a much more penetrating study in depth. Though Johannes Faust
was not born in Prague, he at least had a
stopping-off point there which continues to be
pointed out today yet. Goethe may have
known something about all this from the
twenty-sixth chapter of the *History of Faust*
(Frankfurt, 1587) which appeared during
the residence in Prague of the alchemist Emperor Rudolph II. In the description of the
third magic journey of the black artist Faust
Prague is also described with topographic
thoroughness.

> This capital city in Bohemia is large and di-
> vided into three parts, namely, Old Prague,
> New Prague, and Little Prague. The latter is
> on the left bank with the royal court and the
> St. Vitus Cathedral. Old Prague (the inner
> city) lies on the plain. One gets from there

to Little Prague (Kleinseite) via a bridge
with twenty-four arches. New Prague is separated from Old Prague by a deep ditch
[Later street name: *Graben* ("ditch," Czech
příkopy).] and is also encompassed by a wall
for protection. The College of the High School
is located here.

(To wit, the first mid-European university
founded by Emperor Charles IV in 1348.)
So much for the *History of Faust.* Prague appears there only as a stopping-off point. The
homunculus, the mannikin in the second part
of Goethe's *Faust* is not created by Faust but
by his assistant Wagner, but actually Homunculus derives from the experimental world of
the sixteenth-century alchemists who lived in
Prague. In 1616 Paracelsus actually provided
in *De generatio rerum naturalium* a practical
recipe for the creation of homunculi. The experiences of the Prague alchemists were immediately preceding. (Rudolph II died in
1612.) Thus Prague was the city of a man-
creating mysticism, from which in the course
of time neither the Czech nor German poets of
Prague could divorce themselves, all the less
so because the Jewish Golem legend became a
magical counterpart to the "scientific alchemists." Among the more recent Czech writers
Karel Čapek become world famous by means
of his science-fiction drama *R.U.R.* (*Rossum's*

126

Universal Robots) in which as early as 1923 synthetic modern automatons appeared, called *robots*, a very popular and now world-wide designation derived from Czech *robota* meaning "enforced labor." The forebear of these robots was the Golem of the Prague Rabbi Liwa ben Bezalel of Renaissance times, the High Rabbi Loew. I am not hesitant to claim this dark ancestral heritage for Kafka's *The Metamorphosis* inasmuch as the ceaseless experimental search for the philosopher's stone foreshadows by its persistence and frustration Kafka's everlasting search for security. If one objected that seeking gold is actually seeking power, then the rejoinder should be that power-seeking is actually nothing but an overcompensation for the deepest anxiety and insecurity. If alchemy is the haven of dissatisfied and despairing men within the established religions, then the Emperor Rudolph II was all that.

Goethe researchers will frown upon my conjecture that the magic of the Golem may also have rubbed off onto Goethe, who had been in Bohemia seventeen times though never in Prague, and who when he wrote *The Sorcerer's Apprentice* (*Der Zauberlehrling*) in 1797 may already have gathered together numerous items of local import from spa guests from Prague during his three summers

(1785, 1786, and 1795) at Karlsbad. Nothing about this is documented, to be sure, but his observations about Bohemia in these years are sparse to the point of not existing at all and the thesis *quod non est in actis, non est in mundo* seems highly materialistic to me in the investigation of intellectual-spiritual processes. Goethe had in later years personally received from friends such as the Jewish bankers Leopold and Simon von Lämmel of Prague detailed reports about the Jews of Prague, their oldest synagogs and their famous cemetery, in which the High Rabbi Loew is buried. All that is, indeed, already *in actis* and Goethe remarked in this connection that the cemetery ought to be specially designated and its inscriptions preserved. But why on the occasion of his earlier visits should his Prague informers have suppressed the Golem of all things, one of the poetically most exciting and interesting motifs? Does it seem to be anything but pure coincidence that the Jewish robot of the Renaissance accomplishes the same things and engages in similar monkeyshines and house cleanings as does Goethe's magic broom? Now, Germanistic scholarship derives *The Sorcerer's Apprentice* directly from Lucian, in whose *The Lover of Lies* (*Philopseudes*) an Egyptian priest by means of a magic formula transforms a broom into an

Interior of Old Synagogue, Prague. (Photo, courtesy, The Bettmann Archive, New York.)

River Moldau (*Vltava*), Hradschin Castle and the St. Vitus Cathedral in the background. (Photo, courtesy, Prof. Johannes Urzidil.)

indefatigable servant. These were, indeed, ancient stories, but now hear who brought them
to Goethe. None other than his Hebrew teacher
Albrecht. One should also consider that the
Syrian Lucian did not live too far from the
Jewish mainland where there were some very,
very old traditions regarding the synthetic
creation of man. The substance of these
sources was communicated far and wide beyond all national boundaries and bubbled on
through the Middle Ages and into the Renaissance and Baroque periods. They reappear
with the Arab Avicenna as well as with Al-
bertus Magnus, in Reuchlin's *Cabala* as also
in Schudt's *Remarkable Judaica* of 1714.
Hence, it is possible that the Egyptian priest
was Lucian's source in the latter's *The Lover
of Lies;* conversely, it is also possible that the
Egyptian learned his tricks from a cabalist.

The Jews are documented as being in
Prague as far back as Romanic times. As a
matter of fact, the earliest travel report about
Prague was by a Jew, Abraham ben Jacob,
who in the second half of the tenth century
travelled through Bohemia and the Slavic
countries and recorded his observations in the
Book of Roads and Countries (Codex of Cor-
dova). Already even then he described Prague
as an extremely lively east-west and north-
south crossroads, as a diversified metropolis.

129

The powerfully pulsating city brought forth its myths (such as that of Duchess Libussa, its founder) and the myths in turn created the city. The Golem legend is an integral part of this mythical residue of Prague. The Hebrew word *golem* designates a lifeless formless substance. Golem is not a name but a designation for a thing. Egon Erwin Kisch, one of the most prolific Prague journalists and writers, once insisted that he had sought out the attic of the Old-New-Synagog and there discovered the remains of the Golem. But what Kisch, whose reportorial audacity should not be called into question, probably discovered was crumbled and dried-out remnants of clay, that is to say, *golem*. It would be hard to prove whether these clay remnants were actually the remains of the High Rabbi Loew's synthetic man.

The legend itself has its roots in the earliest of cabalistic works, the *Yetzirah*, to which the Babylonia Talmud already bears witness. The aforementioned work (in the tract *Sanhedrin*) contains a report about the possibilities of infusing life into chaotic substance, to wit, into *golem*. The cabalists believed that the chosen one could infuse life not only into *golem* but also into a human corpse by affixing the *shem*, that is, the scripted symbol of the divine name, on the forehead or under the

130

tongue. The spirit, that is life, is of course omnipresent and indestructible, whereas matter is only the substratum of spirit-life, and so the chosen one can under certain circumstances always relate to the spirit and reinfuse life into what appears to be only dead matter. Who now is chosen and what are the pre-conditions?

Golem myths were issuing forth from Prague already in the Middle Ages but especially during the sixteenth century when the city became the podium and action sphere of the wise Rabbi Liwa ben Bezalel, to whom above all the ability was accorded to be the master of space and matter and consequently also of time. The life and work of Rabbi Liwa have been described in a book by Friedrich Thieberger which till now has appeared only in English. I am adopting the findings of this book by my brother-in-law as a basis for my present study. Thieberger had been occupied with the theme of his book most of his life. I heard him talk about it many times and there is no doubt that in his close relationship to Kafka he thoroughly discussed with him especially this highly significant Golem myth which deeply affected all inhabitants of Prague. Obviously, this simultaneous transience into the super-sensuous against a background of realism and rooted in the religious would prove

extraordinarily fascinating to Kafka. The best
known and most visible historical witness of
the High Rabbi Loew is his already aforementioned tombstone bedecked with many inscriptions in the Jewish cemetery of Prague,
where he lies buried since 1609 surrounded
by the graves of his thirty-three best beloved
students as if by a body guard. Whence Liwa
or Loew came to Prague is uncertain. It is
said that he was born in Posen in Silesia and
that he was still so hale and hearty in his
hundred-and-fourth year that the angel of
death dared not approach him directly but
had instead to disguise himself in the scent
of a rose. Loew's magical powers continued
on, however, even after his death. For when
they sought to bury his grandson beside him
sixty years later only to discover that sufficient land about his grave was not available,
the Rabbi moved over a couple of yards during the night together with his monument.

According to the cabala magical power presupposes three conditions: First, religious impeccability, which in the Jewish view requires
an enormous measure of God's grace for fulfillment, a measure of grace available only to
a chosen one who has already dedicated his
whole life to the spirit of religion; second, an
exclusively spiritual development or education, which though a mere man has the power

for choosing it, requires that he must nevertheless be a comprehending intellect-spirit who
can apply the rare ability of making value
distinctions with respect to all phenomena and
all conditions; last but certainly not least, because it is the chief basis of all the preceding, the profoundest knowledge of the word of
God, that is, of the Torah and the Talmud.
That kind of knowledge implies, however, a
tremendous expenditure of soul absorption, so
intense and so continuous that it comprehends
the rest of life within itself and transmutes
the existence of an adept into eternal learning. The very first step but also the most important is a knowledge of Hebrew. And Kafka
made an attempt at this first step by commencing instruction in Hebrew with Thieberger.
Now, tradition asserts that all three of the
great provisos, which according to the cabala
are requisite for developing supersensuous
powers, were gloriously combined in the
High Rabbi Liwa ben Bezalel. We have to
presuppose his religious impeccability as
something given; his spiritual-intellectual maturation and his knowledge of doctrine are
corroborated by the large number of significant Jewish writings he left. They are, to be
sure, hard to understand and would by their
very nature prove mysterious to every non-
Jew. Some of them bear very impressive and

poetically suggestive titles such as *The Dance of the Righteous, The Hard Heart of Pharaoh, The Tears of God.* In his capacity of head of the congregation Rabbi Loew was self-evidently also its highest judge from whose verdict there could be no appeal. But his judgments were regarded as truly Solomonic and motivated by the highest ethics of the scriptures and the wisest humaneness. He was an astonishing psychologist, who regarded sin as "disorder of the soul" and not as a primitive consequence of spontaneous badness; he was a profound theologian, who recognized in "Jacob's wrestling with the angel the wrestling of the incorporeal in Jacob with an incorporeal messenger of God"; and he was —amidst the sixteenth century—a surprisingly philosophic-theoretic physicist who proclaimed: "Time is but a form of matter and consists of movement." That really was something!

That the Emperor Rudolph up there in the Hradschin, this worrisome reflective seeker of the truth, collector, patron of the arts, and experimentalist should take notice of and want to learn to know this famous *zadik* in the depths of the city was probably to be expected. Contemporary reports exist about the meetings between the two and also about the fact that the Emperor took instruction from the Rabbi. Obviously, a saga-cycle was bound to arise about such meetings. Thus, the Rabbi was once said to have brought the imperial gardens into bloom in the middle of winter. Another time he was reported to have conjured up the Jewish patriarchs at the wish of the Emperor. (We are reminded of a similar exorcism in *Faust* and in *Macbeth.*) Once, when the Emperor went to visit the Rabbi in his modest dwelling, the master of the house suddenly transformed it into a large and luxurious hall. Regardless of all such legends, however, the fact of the relationship and its enormous singularity persists. There was, indeed, the Emperor, and there was, indeed, the Rabbi, their characters are sharply defined in history, and we are as well informed about Liwa ben Bezalel through the medium of his writings and his achievements as about any other man of the time. "Nothing really exists except miracles," Kafka once said. The spirit world is not closed to us as we learn from Goethe's *Faust*. Magic power is always a power of transmuting. The snow-covered garden bursts into bloom. The scholar's study becomes an exotic salon. Time and space are overcome and the patriarchs appear on the scene just as Helena does in *Faust*. Magic is up to the point of abstraction enhanced realism. Animals talk. Dead matter comes alive.

A human being becomes an insect. Basically
there is nothing new, only very ancient fairy-
tale-reality and parable-reality and wisdom.
Who else should possess them except the
Rabbi? And to whom should he convey them,
if not to the Emperor? And Franz Kafka,
come to think of it, ought really not lie buried
in the modern graveyard in Strašnice above
Prague but in the old one alongside the favorite students of the High Rabbi Liwa ben Bezalel. Had one tried to bury him there, the
great teacher would doubtless have moved
aside to make room for him.

The authentic report about the Golem we
have from the hand of the Rabbi's son-in-law,
Yitzchak Bin Simson Cohen, who personally
assisted in the construction and vivification
of the synthetic man. His report says: "We
clothed him with everything a servant of the
synagog required. He then continued sitting
in a corner of the court, head in hands. The
people in the streets looked upon him as a
poor, dumb human being whom the High
Rabbi had adopted out of pity." A poor,
dumb human being in a corner of a courtyard, head in hands. Breitgasse (Broadstreet)
No. 911. The vivified clump of earth saw,
heard and understood everything but he just
could not speak. "He had a body and a real
head and thus also a forehead so he could

136

beat it with his hand." (Kafka). Silent symbol of exposed defenselessness. He hewed
wood, swept floors, wandered many a stretch
to fetch water. However, he was not merely
matter vivified; for he could be invited into
service in a prayer group as the prescribed
tenth male, though only in a silent role, a
"dumb servant," but much, much more than a
mere mechanized broom. His responsibilities
were much more extensive, for his chief obligation was to restrain acts of violence
against Jews. His mere appearance could
even have a sobering effect on pogromists the
lack of whom Prague at no time suffered from
regardless of whether its principal inclination
happened to be Catholic, Hussite or Protestant. *Mažte židi!*—Thrash the Jews!—happens
not to be a translation from the German; for
the present writer was compelled to hear this
battlecry often enough in the streets of Prague
when he was a child and youth, that is, a
good three hundred years after Emperor Rudolph II reigned and some forty years prior
to the Nazi occupation of the city.

As was proper, the Golem had to rest on
the holy sabbath. The Rabbi deactivated his
superhuman powers by removing the *shem*,
the magical formula, he ordinarily carried
under his tongue. *Shem*, more precisely *shem
ha-meforasch*, simply means "the name" and

is the designation for the unspoken and un-
speakable name of God, the phonetic notation
of which is the tetragram *JHWH* coined by
Philo of Alexandria, to wit, Jahweh. Together
with the Jewish congregation the Golem by
resting participated in the most important of
Jewish celebrations, the weekly sanctification
of the sabbath. Even when on such a day acts
of violence against Jews occurred, he could
not succour them. But every legend, to completely legitimatize itself, requires human
weakness as a spice, indeed as a motivating
force. And so it is told that the very wise
Rabbi once forgot on a sabbath to remove the
shem from the Golem. Whereupon the latter
went berserk and knocked everything topsy-
turvy, not just because he seemed to have
been deprived of participating in the observ-
ance embracing everything Jewish, but because he was angered that his master should
for a single moment have failed to be masterful. The people ran to the Old-New-Synagog
where the Rabbi was just commencing to sing
the sabbath psalm. Disturbed by the commo-
tion and by what had transpired the High
Rabbi interrupted the ceremony and hurried
home to divest the Golem of the *shem* and
thus tranquilize him. He then returned to the
synagog and continued with the ceremony. After the events of that sabbath the aforemen-

tioned psalm has always been sung twice in the Old-New-Synagog of Prague.

The end of the Golem is related to a political act of Rudolph II, who by special edict proscribed violence against Jews. The High Rabbi, who certainly had helped to bring about the Emperor's benevolence, thereupon decided to re-transmute his synthetic assistant back to lifeless matter, to *golem,* again. This act entailed not only the divesting of the *shem* but also—as was the case in the original vivification—a special ceremony at which the Rabbi's son-in-law again assisted. Thereupon the two laid the remains of the de-animated matter to rest on the attic floor of the Old-New-Synagog. The remains lay there unnoticed for two centuries. Not till the end of the eighteenth century did the very conservative Rabbi Ezekiel ben Judah Landau of Prague (1713–1793) venture to approach the mystic Golem again after having fasted and donned his death-robe. However, he kept silent about what he had seen and issued a solemn edict forbidding anyone to enter the attic of the synagog in the future.

Egon Erwin Kisch, a daring reporter, who always doted on violating prohibitions, also paid no heed to this one. One of the Arconauts, Fürth, fond of exhibiting his inquisitive curiosity, asked Kisch over a cup of coffee: "And had you previously fasted and donned your shroud for your interview with the Golem?" Whereupon Kisch seemed flabbergasted and may for the first time in his life have been embarrassed. "Well, then it is impossible for you to have seen the Golem," the questioner continued drily. That was no mere sarcasm. In it lay the profound truth that it is possible to perceive and to comprehend only in the state of sanctification. And thus Kafka also spoke of "writing as a form of prayer."

FK

MEMORIALS

If one looked upon Rudolph Fuchs (born
1890 in the historic Central Bohemian town
of Poděbrad, died a victim of the London
blackout of 1942) as merely belonging to
the peripheral Prague acquaintances of
Kafka, one would fail to do justice to the
significance of this relationship. From a literary point of view he was much more interesting to Kafka than, for example, the
dramatic expressionist Paul Kornfeld, a native of Prague, or even the novelist and es-

sayist Ernst Weiss, native of Brünn, both of them widely known in their day and renowned authors, and both—like Fuchs—close friends of mine. (Kornfeld perished in the Nazi concentration camp in Lodz; Weiss, who played a special part in the personal life of Kafka, died a suicide in Paris whose occupation by Hitler's hordes he regarded as the end of Europe.)

Now, Fuchs was especially noted as a literary phenomenon by virtue of the social aspect of his publications. He was a perfect instance of complete bilingualism who could have distinguished himself equally well as a Czech or a German writer but who chose to emphasize the German part of himself in his creative efforts. The nature of his bilingualism was extraordinary inasmuch as he absorbed already when he was first learning to talk, words and their referants, concepts and their meanings in both languages and not by adding the superstructure of a second language to an original foundational linguistic basis. There were other literary phenomena of this kind in Prague, for example, Otto Pick or Paul Eisner, who like Fuchs seemed predestined by nature for the role of liaison and who fulfilled their function as translators in this area in an exemplary manner.

But Fuchs possessed the finest creative tal-

ent of all. He was distinguished by a subtle
solidity, a confident sensitivity already recognizable in his first little book of lyric poems
published in Heidelberg in 1913 under the
title *Der Meteor* (*The Meteor*) in Hermann
Meister's publishing house "Saturn." Because
of this title Werfel was wont to call Fuchs
the "cosmic poet." The latter, however, manifested himself as much more earthy and hu-
manely aware than "cosmic." A second volume of feet-on-the-ground lyrics followed in
1918 under the title *Karawane* (*Caravan*).
The third collection was his swan's song. It
appeared in 1941 "owing to the generosity
of a friend" shortly before his death in England in an edition of 140 copies and was entitled *Poems from Reigate* after the name of
his refuge in exile.

Fuchs achieved real significance, even
fame as a result of his admirable translations
of the astonishing lyric poems, hewn from
stone as it were, of the Czech-Silesian miner-
poet Petr Bezruč (his family name was Vlad-
imír Vašek) [Translator's note: Petr Bezruč's *Silesian Songs* has just recently appeared in an English translation by Ian Mil-
ner, Prague: Artia, 1967.], which appearing
in Czech under the title *Slezské písně* (*Silesian Songs*) ominously proclaimed the hot
anger and rebelliousness of a national minor-

ity, oppressed nationally as well as socially
in their beloved and abused homeland. Here
lay the motive power that had to effect Kafka
deeply, for he had already become professionally concerned about the destiny and trib-
ulations of the workers and was disquieted
and even suffered mental torture as a result.
Bezruč did not seem to any of us to be a
poetic personality so much as a social phenomenon in the same way that Walt Whitman
seemed to be the universal great voice of
democratic America rather than a specific
lyric poet, or as Gerhard Hauptmann's *Die
Weber* (*The Weavers*) seemed less a drama
than the despairing outcry of an anonymous
group of suffering human beings who had
been deprived of all rights. Consequently also
Franz Werfel in the foreword to the first edition of Fuchs' translation of *Silesian Songs*
(published by Kurt Wolff in Leipzig in 1916)
characterized the poet Petr Bezruč not as a
man but rather as a kind of mythical agglom-
eration of "the anger of free speech." "Petr
Bezruč does not exist. He is the instrument
of exiled powers, the chosen one of angry,
long vanquished, ancient gods, who in a last
effort gathered themselves together in force
and began to howl in mortal pain above the
heads of the disintegrating sibling-groups."
True, Bezruč could be understood only as

the impersonal outcry of a persecuted group
of human beings. Fuchs said of him (he could
be specifically identified only later), he was
"a poet against his will"; his poetry was a
resounding outcry from the shafts and pits of
the mines in Ostrava and Teschen and the
forests of the Beskids, a roar of rage against
the mine owners and also the "Marquis Gero"
who—as everyone knew—was the hated Austrian Archduke Frederick, lord of the lands
and commander-in-chief of the imperial
armies during the First World War. Bezruč's
overpowering effect seemed to Fuchs even
more vehement than that of François Villon,
which was also directed against the money
and power mongers of his age. Incidentally,
the land of origin of the author of *Silesian
Songs* was the same as that of the great com-
poser Leos Janáček who became known to
world audiences through the efforts of Max
Brod.

"I, Petr Bezruč of Teschen," sounded for-
sooth like "Walt Whitman, a Kosmos, of Man-
hattan the son" except that it lacked the jubi-
lation of the songs of the American. Bezruč's
tone was instead despairing, hopeless, deeply
incensed about the need and the mutilation
of the miners, about the Germanizing and
Polonizing of the Czechs in these regions, and
about the financial exploitation on the part

of German-speaking Christians and Jews.
The anti-Semitic overtones prevailing throughout the *Silesian Songs* should not be understood as such but rather as a grim social
protest sweeping everything before it without
distinction. After all, it was significant that
Bezruč was translated into German and was
introduced to a wider public by Fuchs, who
was a Jew, and Werfel, also a Jew, wrote an
enthusiastic foreword to this translation. I
had been corresponding with Bezruč (incidentally, he wrote to me in German, which
was by no means his custom, and I regarded
this fact as an unusual distinction) but I
never felt that I was in the presence of someone I could describe as a literary or poetic
personality. He seemed rather to be an erratic
monolith. What occasioned the correspon-
dence was Bezruč's love of the German poet
and nay-sayer Friedrich Hölderlin.

Now, when Fuchs published his German
translation of *Silesian Songs* in the middle of
the First War (the Czech original had appeared in 1903), the effect was literally that
of a cataclysm, an invitation to demonstrative
partisanship, an accusing engagement with
the powers that were. Though Fuchs was by
nature delicate and sublime, quiet and re-
strained in his personal relations, he was not
—as was apparent—a sneak. It is not neces-

sary here to regurgitate again Kafka's own frequently discussed social position to explain why Fuchs moved him so deeply both as a poet in his own right but especially as the German-speaking herald of Bezruč.

In the addenda to his biography of Kafka, Max Brod published an observation by Fuchs about his connection with Kafka, which began in the famous Café Arco and came to an end with Kafka's burial. Fuchs and I walked away from Kafka's covered grave silent and deeply moved. What was there still to say? We knew we were now orphaned. Not till a few hours later in Fuchs's small dwelling did we regain speech to talk not about our loss but about the simple things around us, a vase, a mug, a chest, for such things could still be discussed of a certainty inasmuch as the great creative constant was gone. For this was what Kafka had been to us—even if he did not so regard himself—and despite all of the aphoristic and fragmentary character in his life as well as in his works. Both of us postponed many another sorrow for later on. I am certain, however, no other grieving was so unconditional and so profound.

I always had the feeling of platinum in the presence of Fuchs, of something cool and high-grade. Inasmuch as he was native to a

completely Czech small town, his German retained a more noticeable coloration of Czech
accent than was the case with the Prague Germans, who amidst the Czech majority dwelt
within a predominantly German-speaking
group. Incidentally, Kafka's speech resembled
that of Fuchs more than of his other Prague
literary friends. However, the tonality of
Kafka's speech might have had a family connection, for his parents had retained the un-
mistakable tone of the Czech province whence
they came. The appearance of *Silesian Songs*
in German in 1916 had a tremendous impact,
which Fuchs transmitted to all of us, and
which from the first moments of the War had
represented a protest against power and
against militarism, against every kind of
chauvinism and of the persecution of linguistic or religious minorities. None of the Prague
German authors in our circle ever found it
necessary to revise his political views as did
many a leading German author, whose conscience did not remonstrate till the war had
been lost for its instigators, its propagandists
and enthusiastic proponents, and till the zeal-
ous creators of war almanacs and the admirers of the violators of neutrality had once
again to reckon with the new reality of defeat. I offer this observation not as an accusation but rather as something regrettable, be-

cause it did separate us Praguers in marked fashion from other German-language writers whom we were accustomed to venerate, just as later we had to rip the much adored Knut Hamsun from our hearts as a person and thereby only increase our misery as a result of our persistent admiration for his writings. It is not merely that we continue fervently to wish that literary artist we admire would also share our moral views, but rather that we suffer from seeming to disavow our best and most important views and thus to go astray, so that we have to fight to regain them again even against our own idols. And so in my address at the Prague memorial service for Kafka (1924) I related Kafka to Knut Hamsun (for Kafka adored him) and thus showed up Kafka in a community which later became so dreadfully suspect because of the attitude of the great Norwegian writer.

Fuchs translated not only Bezruč. The Czechs are also obligated to him for transmitting many another lustrous emission of their poetry as are the Germans for poetic encounters they would not have had except for Fuchs. In cooperation with Paul Eisner, Jan Loewenbach, Otto Pick and others, Fuchs made available a whole series of translations of modern Czech authors in a collection entitled *Recent Czech Lyric Poems,* published

by the Berlin literary review *Die Aktion* (edited by Franz Pfemfert) toward the end of
1916. Obviously, this was also an audacious
effort in the middle of the War. For the Czechs
were regarded in the nationalistic German
lump judgment as traitors to the Austro-
Hungarian monarchy and from the time of
the German playwright Friedrich Hebbel on
as a nation of servants whose "culture" was
not worth discussing, that is, a people (according to an impudent verse of Hebbel re-
viling Stifter) capable of nothing except "to
shake their unkempt caryatidal heads." *Die
Aktion* was at that time the rallying point of
the expressionists and of the oppositional
"angry young men of that period." My own
first poems were appearing in that journal at
that time. Later on Fuchs published a com-
prehensive book of translations called *Ernte-
kranz aus hundert Jahren tschechischer Dichtung (Harvest Wreath from a Century of
Czech Literary Art)*, a publication Kafka did
not live to see.

When the young man Rudolf Fuchs came
to Prague from the town of Poděbrad to complete his studies in the German secondary
school, he lived at first with the Thieberger
family and became friends with the two
daughters of the house, Nelly and the younger
Trude. In 1939 my wife Trude and I met

150

him and his wonderful wife Loni in exile in London. They shared the tragedy, common to so many fugitives, of living less from bread than from the sullen conviction that the dark forces of power would still ultimately have to disintegrate. None of the three authors from Prague and Bohemia, who were my friends and from whom I took leave in London when it was my good fortune in 1941 to get to the United States in dramatic fashion, Rudolph Fuchs, Ludwig Winder, and Ernst Sommer, ever saw their homeland again. All of them wrote to me regularly in New York but they died in exile in London. Winder and Sommer at least lived to the end—or should we say the preliminary conclusion?—of hostilities but Fuchs was the victim of an accident during the blackout and bombardment of London. Loni outlived him by only a few months. To her, but not only to her, he wrote his last verses.

Mach kein trauriges Gesicht—
Auf den Feldern dieses schlechten Krieges
grünen schon die Reiser unseres Sieges.
Ruhig brennt das Licht.

Gute Nacht, und bange nicht!
Eine große Macht geht nicht mehr schlafen,
wacht in jeder Stadt, in jedem Hafen.
Ohne sie ist kein Gedicht.

Ohne sie kein Tag mehr, keine Nacht.
Tiefer schweigt die Brust, 's ist Feierabend.
Du auch bist ein Teil der großen Macht,
die in jedem Dorf, in jedem Hafen wacht.

[Do not look sad—the sprouts of our victory are already beginning to green on the battlefields of this bad war. The light burns calmly.

Good night and be not afraid! A great power will not fall asleep again but wakes in every city, in every harbor. Without this power there is no poem.

Without this power there is no longer a day or a night.

One's heart becomes more silent, it's eventide.

You too are part of the great power,
Watching in every village, every harbor.]

One would look in vain for information about Ernst Feigl in any literary reference work. His name occurs several times in Kafka's letters. He may have been a year or two older than I, he withstood the varicolored horrors of the age in Prague, and died there in 1964. We saw each other regularly and before his marriage I also visited him oc-

casionally in his parents' home where he lived
with his busy sisters, a near shabby courtyard apartment in an old house in New
Prague (Nové Město), called New Town
though already founded in Gothic times. The
house had the same mustiness peculiar to
Brand's house on the Kleinseite below the
Castle Hill, it smelled of chicory, softsoap,
pregnant cats, cave-ins, rotten timbers, and
the mysterious contents of trunks in endless
attics. I know nothing of Feigl's father's business but it could not have been lucrative.
All three sons, Friedrich, Hugo, and Ernst
were artistically talented to a marked degree.
Friedrich, the oldest, soon became recognized
as an extraordinary painter, a master of
graphics and black-and-white drawings, who
was highly regarded by both Germans and
Czechs and later enjoyed a like recognition
in Berlin and London where he died in 1966.
He made a sketch of Kafka while the latter
was doing a reading, a powerful portrait
which was reproduced in the *Kafka Catalog*
of the Berlin Academy of Art, edited by Klaus
Wagenbach and published in 1966. This life-
sketch reflects a likeness as strong as those
imagined but extraordinarily intuited Kafka
portraits by Hans Fronius do in such an amazing way. Kafka alludes to the painter Fritz
Feigl in a 1916 letter to Kurt Wolff as a

Dostoevsky illustrator for the publisher Georg Müller. The second brother, Hugo Feigl, did not utilize his doctor's degree in the law professionally, but instead and as a labor of love founded an art and exhibit salon in Prague, in which I never saw a mediocre painting or an insignificant sculpture, nothing but exclusively contemporary works of the highest quality and of international repute. In exile in New York he had the strength and tenacity immediately to found a new salon of the same kind and to win for it the renown accorded him there during the last two decades of his life. The third brother, the aforementioned Ernst, who was to be the subject of discussion here, roamed about at random in the sphere of literary art. "Roamed about at random" is perhaps the proper endeavors for he came and went and then came back again. He was a born author of dramatic fragments and worked throughout his life on a theater piece called *Don Juan,* which was so broadly conceived as to make any ending impossible. Such a conception is not unconditionally something to be held against a work of literary art, perhaps it has no validity at all, particularly since from Goethe we know (*Italian Journey*, Caserta, 16 March 1787) that great works of art are never finished but are merely "declared to be finished." Now, how "great" Feigl's *Don Juan* was is hard to say in retrospect. From it the author recited scene after scene to us in the Café Arco, where people were always fond of reciting before grain dealers, promiscuous girls and shady operators. Werfel also engaged in this kind of elocutionist activity. It is likely that Kafka failed to escape one of the *Don Juan* recitals. The archeologists of Prague expressionism may dig up some of the scenes from this drama from Oskar Wiener's anthology *German Poets of Prague*, published in 1919 and illustrated by the painter Friedrich Feigl. Franz Werfel is portrayed therein with youthful long hair alongside of Hugo Salus with the long hair of an old man. Also included are the non-Prague Praguer Gustav Meyrink with the penetrating eyes of a spook registrar, Paul Leppin with the erect proud bearing of a romantic lyricist, Friedrich Adler in the affluence of the "liberal" bourgeois era, and Kafka's good friend (mine also) Oskar Baum, blinded early in life, with his far-reaching Tiresias look. Max Brod, Rudolph Fuchs, Paul Kornfeld, and Ludwig Winder are also represented in this book. I contributed some of my own poems as well as several of the deceased Karl Brand.

Obviously, Ernst Feigl could not make a living with his poems and his interminable drama, and so he finally got a job as a court-room reporter for the *Prager Tagblatt*, a call-ing which appealed greatly to him because it would constantly afford him contact with many and diverse human situations, and with the destinies of right and wrong, of terrible and laughable circumstances, of cowardice and shamelessness. However, one could also encounter human virtues there every day. Feigl fulfilled his reportorial obligations in a human manner focussing on the heart and compassion of his readers by means of that kind of humor which illuminates human in-adequacy in a comforting kind of way. But Feigl's daemon, which pursued him through-out his life, was his *Don Juan,* a combination of Lorenzo da Ponte and Frank Wedekind.

I once heard him reciting from the play in a women's club in Prague:

> Ich sah dich schon vom Weiten strahlen.
>> Näher Weib!
> Du spanntest Gier vor deinen Leib.
> Du sollst mich betten, Weib,
> Und dein Hütte ist ein Fürstenschloß
> und Fürstin ist dein Leib.

[I already saw you glittering from afar. Come nearer, Woman! You hitched desire up to your body.

> You shall bed me, Woman,
> And your hut is a prince's castle,
> And princess is your body.]

156

How strange! And moreover in Masaryk's republic which had eliminated the nobility. The ladies who had just been knighted in this fashion decided instead of the gratification to plant an olive tree in the Holy Land. Feigl expressed his thanks and said: "But you can also add a couple of cans of sardines in olive oil for me."

The *Prager Tagblatt,* for which he later wrote his courtroom reports under the by-line *ei* ("egg": "I lay my egg daily"), was a fluorescent institution with the best news service in Prague and with an excellent editorial staff not only of versatile journalists but occasionally also of name-authors and even literary artists (such as Berthold Viertel, Max Brod, Rudolph Fuchs). The editor Dr. Rudolf Keller was an important scholar and a world renowned biochemist. When speaking of Kafka, we must also expend a few words on this newspaper. Not only did he personally know most of the editors, he read the paper daily and got from it most of his information which probably colored the reality of his image of the world and his writings about it not a little. I said that the *Prager Tagblatt* was "fluorescent" because it was neither for nor against the Germans, neither for nor against the Czechs, neither for nor against the Christians, neither for nor against the Jews, neither for nor against the

socialists; in a word it was a "liberal" newspaper with the homely motto: "I just like
everybody," except he be opposed to freedom
of speech and approve any kind of censorship. The readers of the *Prager Tagblatt* were
predominantly German-Jewish though the
paper—the largest in Bohemia—also reached
a considerable number of Czechs who could
read German, whereas the second German-
liberal and competing daily *Bohemia,* though
much older, was limited almost exclusively
to German readers and liked to assume, if
not a German-nationalist, then a definitely
"more nationalistic" tone which was a little
less friendly to the Czechs. It is nonetheless
significant that the first works of Kafka published from 1909–1910 in Prague (*The Aero-
planes at Brescia, On the Tram, Reflections
for Gentlemen-Jockeys*) appeared in *Bohemia.* That happened, to be sure, far back
in the days of old Austria, in which the op-
positions and differences, regardless of how
real they were, were nevertheless covered and
made ambiguous by the deceptive umbrella
of the monarchy. Karl Kraus had been publishing *Die Fackel* already since 1899, but
the battle of this Viennese, native of Jičin in
Bohemia, against yellow journalism had not
yet aroused the literary world at the turn of
the century as deeply as it would later. And

so I must also include among the sins of my
youth the fact that I functioned on the editorial staff of the *Prager Tagblatt* several
months after Czechoslovakia had been established. I was assigned to doing short fillers
about local events and my greatest triumph
was an article about Czech barbers, who had
painted their signs (glittering brass bowls
like the famous helmet of Don Quixote) red-
blue-white in an outburst of nationalist feeling. My comment: "Excessively political barbers are often a sign of over-tonsorialized
politics." I was still permitted to go that far
at that time with critical implications. However, because they feared I might become even
more pointed, the end of my practical activi-
ties in the circle of rotational machines was
at hand.

I cannot recall whether Kafka read the
courtroom reports over the by-line "ei." But
he knew about Feigl even before the latter
joined the editorial staff of the *Prager Tagblatt*. As regards *Don Juan,* Kafka may have
taken refuge in the same old cautious-aston-
ished ruse he often employed: "No. I would
never be able to achieve a thing like that."
But Feigl's poems were quite another matter.
They appealed to Kafka as early as 1915.
He wrote the author that these poems evidenced an impenetrable combination of hope

and despair whereby they seemed to have something thoroughly invigorating. His remark did, however, carefully emphasize his own "inadequacy respecting poems." Now, there is no question that Kafka was obviously and totally a prose writer, to whom lyric structuring might seem a sort of pretext for the reality of felt experience and thought (possibly also dramatic structuring, wherein I at least incline to think his prose could never eventually be cast); but that he was unable to distinguish good lyric poetry from bad would be a nonsensical assumption. What he wrote Feigl about the latter's poems was neither an evasion nor a concession conditioned by human consideration. He believed what he said and even recommended Feigl's poems for inclusion in Kurt Wolff's famous booklet series *Der jüngste Tag* (*The Last Day*). He even phrased his recommendation strongly and not at all like those routine recommendations others write to rid themselves of an onerous obligation toward authors requesting recommendations. These poems, so he wrote, would constitute "a substantial enrichment" of the series, for Feigl still has "powerful, by far still unarticulated possibilities within himself." (Kafka's letters to Kurt Wolff regarding Feigl's poetry have been published in their entirety in Kurt Wolff, *Brief-*

wechsel eines Verlegers, 1911–1963, Frankfurt a. M.: Scheffler, 1966.)

This recommendation did not, however, have the desired result. Five Prague writers, Oskar Baum, Max Brod, Franz Kafka, Franz Werfel, and myself, are represented in the eighty-six volumes of *The Last Day* published between 1913 and 1921. (In this connection see the two summary volumes published by Paul Raabe, viz., *Expressionismus, Katalog der Ausstellung des Schiller National-Museums,* 1960, and *Expressionismus, Aufzeichnungen und Erinnerung der Zeitgenossen,* 1965.)

And now a Prague scherzo! There are litterateurs who never achieve anything literary, at least nothing printed, but who by virtue of their wandering about or sitting about in the literary area, by their talk or perceptible thought, by astonishing remarks, actions, or conduct exercise a certain influence which can vary in strength from person to person and be more powerful than written or printed observations. There was quite a number of such persons in Prague. The overly erudite Ernst Pollak was that kind of person, a totally uncreative yet highly regarded cynic, a stupendously clever fellow who always knew more and knew it better, an all-around jack-of-all-literary trades, intellectual bank official, sharpeyed, small in stature but successfully mimicking Balzac's Rastignac as to the art of living, who was fallen upon by a whole bunch of beautiful and lovable, even very clever women, among them also the glorious Milena Jesenská, whom we all regarded as a miracle, the deeply beloved of Kafka and the woman to whom he wrote his most fascinating love letters.

Another such sideliner was Otto Rosenfeld, who owned an exquisite little coffeeshop but in addition was at all times extraordinarily witty. He managed to get into print, however, by means of little newspaper notices which he signed as "Roeld" after he first— so one said—had eliminated the *senf* ("mustard") not only from his name but also from his story. He even succeeded with a lot of help in publishing a novel *Malenski auf der Tour (Malenski on Tour)*, the collective misfortunes of a drummer by the name of Malenski retained in talented fashion, simply because the author did everything he undertook with a certain talent regardless of whether it had to do with a coffeehouse, the playful improvising of spoonerisms or the parodying of Franz Werfel's poems. To be sure, he never dared, nor would it ever have occurred to him, to want to parody, say, Kafka. What Rosenfeld always avoided, namely respect, this even he accorded Kafka sincerely and unconditionally.

The most scurrilous personality among the Prague litterateurs devoid of literature was without doubt Walter Fürth. He was two or three years my junior but his manner, or rather lack of it, captivated me to such an extent that I asked that excellent painter Egon Adler, then (1918) living in Prague, to paint me a portrait of this unique fellow, a request my friend gladly granted me gratis. The portrait like many other things has remained in Prague since my flight from there in 1939, and I know not what might have befallen it. In it Fürth looked as he really was, externally and internally, crowned with a gigantic mop of wildly curling hair, much like countless hairsplitting philosophical arguments running confusedly pro and con and all adding up to the opposite of a system, a compact nihilistic entity underneath which glittered a button-nosed Socrates-face, sarcastic and panting for dialog. The face always seemed to be saying: "Nothing will, of course, come from this conversation with you," a distrustful and contemptuous basic attitude toward almost all men. I say, almost. For though I have heard him criticize very nearly all men I have seen in his company, regardless of whether they were writers, rabbis, businessmen or his own parents, he never took Kafka on. Fürth's frankness bordered on shamelessness but with the result that with a sharpness of eye not to be denied he intuited at once the weak points of his discussant and then proceeded pitilessly to tear one mask off him after another. He was not so much intent upon embarrassing the other fellow as he was to lay bare the embarrassment his opponent sought to cover up with shields of seeming security. "Don't deal so confidently with opinions you yourself do not basically subscribe to. Don't try to fool me!" He was a master at driving a person into a corner and once when I happened to be present this nineteen-year-old even tried to rattle Martin Buber who must then have been about forty. But never Kafka.

Fürth nurtured within himself a most uncoordinated confusion corresponding to his coiffure. He was simultaneously a devotee of Hegel and of Schopenhauer, a Spinozist and a neo-Christian, he interceded for Weininger and propagated suicide as a means of eventual escape from the revulsion, dullness, emptiness, and fruitlessness of this utterly senseless

164

life. But everything always remained propaganda. He lived off of death, which he lauded and celebrated in every way. If you asked him: "How are you?" he would without exception reply: "I am suffering." When you then asked: "From what?" the response was: "How can you ask, you dumbbell? Obviously I am suffering from you. For you symbolize the end of man." If you inquired: "Are you at work on something?" he would reply: "Of course. I'm working like mad." To the question: "On what?" the answer: "On a novel." —"Since when?"—"For years."—"How far along are you?"—"The first sentence." And it was apparent that he was about to add: "You jerk!" because he could not understand how a young man might decide to begin a second sentence without fearing—aside from all unfortunate accidents—that even the time required for living a normal happy life was inadequate by far for a first sentence. Fürth may possibly have been the viable burlesque Kafka-image abroad in Prague, unless it was Weissenstein with whom the central story of my *Prager Triptychon* (*Prague Triptychon*) deals but who had less to do with Kafka than Fürth did. Kafka had to meet the latter unavoidably everywhere in the city, not only in the café, which Kafka visited only infrequently, but in every street, lane, and square.

He was everywhere and—in a bizarre way—
apparently everywhere simultaneously. This
simultaneity was a strange phenomenon, common to various persons in Prague, or maybe
it was just that some of us had at our disposal the power of multiple vision. Fürth is
mentioned but once in Kafka's correspon-
dence. Brod may have overlooked Fürth in
connection with Kafka, for only the most
important things were important to him in
that respect. Moreover, Fürth was anything
but an "attractive contemporary" and he had
—as I well know—permitted himself all kinds
of insolences relative to Brod. And Kafka
refrained from noting down the name of many
a person with whom I know for sure he was
acquainted, indeed, to whom he was even at-
tentive. Personal notations are not just fussy
registrations of names and events, in any case
they are rarely that. Among Fürth's best
friends were Friedrich Thieberger and the
philosopher Felix Weltsch, next to Brod one
of Kafka's closest friends. Fürth had the run
of Weltsch's house (I was often there with
him), drank coffee and overwhelmed the
young piano-playing mistress of the house
with aggressive remarks all the while chat-
tering about "grace and freedom" (Felix
Weltsch, *Gnade und Freiheit*) with a vengeance, and intermittently exuding again and

166

again something extremely brilliant. One might regard him as indiscreet, pushy, and in addition physically repugnant but he nevertheless remained an amusing *enfant terrible,* who attracted everyone's attention with his intellectual capers but bored no one.

He also often visited Kafka's good friend Oskar Baum and undertook—just as I did— to take the dear, wonderful blind writer for an occasional walk, to give overburdened Mrs. Baum a little relief. On such occasions Fürth lost his cynicism. "I never see so much as when I go walking with Baum," he said. And it was true. The blind man could in conversation open up the widest perspectives. We loved him dearly. Of all the people in Kafka's milieu he seemed the gayest and most positive and had the nicest faith in life. This may have been the very reason why the negativist Fürth was so attracted to him but would immediately again become the Mephistophelian spirit that denies invariably, and would carry on his usual tirades about the unavoidable destruction of mankind, the futility of all efforts to improve and convert men, hardly tolerable except for certain rare individuals and considered as a group a bunch of jerks who deserve their fate.

"I just met Kafka in the Zeltnergasse."

"What did you talk about?"

"About nothing. I proved to him that mankind is going to pot."

"And what did he say to that?"

"What should he have said? He smiled and shook his head."

"Approvingly or disapprovingly?"

"Both."

When Kafka smiled, it might mean: You are basically right but what's to be done about it?

Fürth, the Ahasverus-like wanderer, was despite all his nihilism continuously involved with founding and preparing for imaginary journals and monthlies which should serve the task of saving the world via literature but no such plans were ever realized.

"Yesterday I suggested to Kafka—the establishment of a new journal."

"What will it be called?"

"Hesperus."

"Why?"

"Stupid question. The same planet that in the evening functions as Hesperus functions as Venus in the morning."

"And so, why not call it Venus?"

"But it is not intended as an erotic journal."

"And what did Kafka have to say about it?"

"He asked, whether I had a patron. And

when I replied 'not just yet,' he suggested
that I might just find myself some rich old
guy with money and forget about publishing a journal."

"What a fine idealism!"

Shortly after the end of the Second World
War Fürth died. Earlier he had sent me a
package in New York. The postman brought
it just as I was about to move and was standing in front of the moving van. I opened the
package and realized immediately that it
contained a manuscript. I was in no position
in my ambivalent situation to do anything
about it immediately except to put it with
our other possessions in the moving van. But
when we unpacked, it was no longer there.
Surely it included the novel, finally completed, which thirty years earlier in the Café
Arco was begun with the sentence: "Walter
F. inherited nothing from his father except
the curse to go on living."

FK

LIFE IS SHORT, ART IS LONG

The concomitance of literary and plastic art is a necessary assumption relative to the period in which Kafka completed his major writings; indeed, frequently the literary and plastic works of art of that period can be understood and explained only in relation to each other. The evidence is twofold, namely, the numerous instances of double talent, that is, talent in more than one artistic medium, on the part of such artists as Alfred Kubin, Oskar Kokoschka, Paul Klee, Lothar Schreyer, Ludwig Meidner, etc., furthermore such publications as *Der blaue Reiter* (1912), Herwarth Walden's *Sturm* or Franz Pfemfert's *Aktion*. A treatment of the significance of plastic art for Kafka must be based on the consideration that he was from childhood on surrounded by an artistically unique city, his eye was accustomed to viewing large forms and architectural products of the romanesque, gothic, and renaissance periods, but especially of the baroque era and the derivative styles thereof. He registered for art history when he first began his university studies, and so he must have become more closely acquainted with Prague's art collections at that time, if not earlier. Though various later journeys (Switzerland, Italy, France, Germany) may have added to his knowledge of art—and we do find many observations, allusions and reactions to art in his notes and writings—his hometown nevertheless remained his most important and constant esthetic source of nourishment. The Charles Bridge, the Theinkirche, the St. Vitus Cathedral, and many another architectural gem of the city provided the obvious as well as the secret settings for many of Kafka's prose pieces.

Heinz Ladendorf's thorough investigation of Kafka's art interests (*Wallraf-Richartz-Jahrbuch*, XXIII and XXV, 1961 and 1963)

includes a treatment of the "constant give and
take between the plastic and literary arts"
so prominent with Kafka, as well as the significance for Kafka's creative processes of
the abundance of art knowledge he seemed
almost to keep secret from himself. Actually,
however, he did not "keep it (completely)
secret." Gustav Janouch reports in his conversations with Kafka that the latter wished
he were able to draw. However, he explained
that Jews were narrators and not painters.
But on another occasion he designated himself (again to Janouch) as being an *Augen-
mensch*, that is, one who perceives life pri-
marily through his eyes rather than his ears
as does an *Ohrenmensch*. Now, it is unquestionably true that plastic art does not represent an aboriginal element of primal Judaism,
to which the decalog already forbade the
forming of images (strictly speaking, any
rhapsodically beautiful object formed by man
is actually an idol per se) and for which
the abstract projection of God could at best
lend itself to decorative purposes but under
no circumstances to figuration. Hans Kohn,
the well known historian and ethnologist and
one of the important Prague figures of the
generation born in the early nineties, con-
fronts Greek culture and Jewish culture in
one of his books thus: "The Greek beholds,

172

the Jew listens." This confrontation conforms
to the words of the biblical prayer introduc-
ing the definition of the Jewish god-relation-
ship: "Hear, oh Israel!" Accordingly, Jewish
musicality has from the time of King David
to the present always been more prominent
than Jewish plastic art though the latter has
since the so-called "emancipation" of Middle
European Jews and the process of assimilation following it grown in importance as has
the number of impressive creative Jewish
personalities in that field. The question must
probably remain moot, whether the aforementioned growth counterbalances the loss in substance resulting from assimilation.

In any case Kafka not only manifested a
definite inclination toward works of plastic
art but was also subject to viable artistic
urges, which are easily documented by means
of a series of available specimens though
many more of these still remain to be dis-
closed. The role which the inclination or talent of a literary artist toward painting and
drawing can play in his creative efforts and
his world view and view of life is evidenced
by persons such as Goethe, Stifter, Keller, or
Hesse, to mention only a few striking ex-
amples. But the significance of association
with plastic art and of the active willing of
authors in the direction of imagizing contin-

ued growing particularly after French impressionism and post-impressionism, which stimulated and transmitted an ever deeper acquaintance with East Asian art, especially with masters of the Japanese woodcut such as Harunobu, Hokusai, Toyokuni, or Hiroshige. No mere artistic-esthetic experience was involved here but rather the discovery of an entirely new and different philosophical worldview corresponding to the simultaneously growing understanding of the work and effect of Laotse, Shang-tse, and Kung-Fu-tse. Individual Praguers were enthusiastically collecting Japanese woodcuts which were diligently discussed in the Café Arco. I acquired my first Toyokuni (which still hangs in my New York apartment) in 1914 from the Prague bookseller Pyšvejc in the Heinrichsgasse (Jindřišská ulice), where Kafka occasionally also browsed about and where, incidentally, stacks of Daumier lithographs were lying around. The interest in East Asian art was consistently followed by an interest in every other kind of exotic and "primitive" art expression, particularly that of Negroes and subsequently of children, and on quite another level the art projections of the mentally ill. Prevailing conceptions of beauty were subjected to scrutiny and revision which resulted in nothing so new and revolutionary as one supposed. After all, had not Goethe already in 1773 in his essay *Von deutscher Baukunst* (*Concerning Gothic Architecture*) uttered the warning: "Art matures a long time before it is beautiful, albeit art, that true and great, is often indeed truer and greater than beauty itself." He was referring to the sculptures of savages, and three decades later Riemer transmits from him the sentence, astonishing for that day and age: "The greatest works of art are plainly displeasing; they are ideals which can and should provide only approximate satisfaction." (Incidentally, this same sentence reappears verbatim in Novalis's *Fragments*.) Goethe had already anticipated in Strassburg what Carl Einstein and Picasso proclaimed 150 years later about Negro sculpture when he said: "For a structuring nature inheres in man. And so the savage structures his cocos, his feathers and his bodies in adventurous terms, horrible shapes and bright colors. And let these creations from the most arbitrary forms be: they will correlate without structural relationship; for a felt perception created them into a characteristic whole." Goethe's views about art, much as they are wont to be denigrated just as his musicality is, manifest in utterances of this kind much more advanced insights than do his contemporaries, wallowing in outmoded esthetics, or than later critics do. But even in our view his judgments seem very modern.

The few drawings of Kafka which have become known till now reveal a definite sense for characterizing features, the working out, for instance, of the basic characteristic of a movement, that is to say, of the "moment of petrifaction," as Goethe expressed it, a trait exemplified—by concentrating within itself all preceding and still forthcoming stages of a movement—in Kafka's *Rider,* the spirited élan of which Ladendorf, incidentally, quite properly compared with the title-symbol of the *Blue Rider.* It is possible that Kafka picked up many an experience regarding movement in Hellerau, near Dresden, where the Dalcroze School was located. I recall the "Studies in Motion," drawn there by the Czech artist Hugo Boettinger, which attracted a certain attention in Prague and with which Kafka was surely acquainted. I was the owner of one of these drawings, depicting my friend the expressionist Prague actress Fritta Brod (later the wife of dramatist Paul Kornfeld). There are certain similarities between Boettinger's characters and Kafka's excited figures. In the main, however, Kafka's drawings suggest the pictographic figures of primitive African tribes, figures whose striking and uninterrupted expression of movement creates a scripto-symbolism, thereby occupying the logical middleground between word and image.

Many parallels and relationships between Kafka's literary universe of images and the plastic art of his day can easily be drawn. Ladendorf has done invaluable pioneer work in this respect, just as he has developed the significance of manneristic art and of the artistic representation of labyrinths to Kafka's forms as well as to his thought processes. The line of development from Kafka to the work of the expressionist graphic artist Alfred Kubin (1877–1959) is corroborated by common biographical dates. Kafka knew this German-Bohemian personally, who originated in Leitmeritz in Central Bohemia (at that time a German-speaking town), and mentions him frequently in the diaries and letters. He had observed him very carefully on various occasions but seems not to have liked him too well as a human being. However, he did regard him highly as an artist. It would seem that Kubin, the masterful portrayer of the grotesque, bizarre, and the "other side" of existence (Kubin's *Die andere Seite*), was influenced more by Kafka than the latter was by Kubin. Kubin also reveals certain affinities to the Russian world of feeling (as was the case also with the German-Praguer Rilke).

The works of the great Russian storytellers from Gogol to Tolstoy had also since the *fin de siècle* begun by means of new translations to exercise their great influence on German readers. The writers learned from them and the graphic artists illustrated them.

The parallels between Kafka and Marc Chagall (born 1887) were drawn by me as long ago as the thirties in the art journal *Forum,* published at that time in Pressburg (Bratislava). My study proceeded on the basis of the Jewish element dominating the two geniuses. I have just now (1965) in a roundabout way acquired a photostatic copy of my study, lost during my escape from Prague. And I am moved to remark that in that study (a discussion of the first Chagall exhibit in Prague in the art salon of Hugo Feigl) I got to mention all of the artists who had significance for Kafka or require mention in connection with him, Kubin of course, but also Hieronymus Bosch, Callot, Goya, E.Th.A. Hoffmann, James Ensor, and Paul Klee. "Kafka too," I wrote at that time, "like the Jewish Marc Chagall, native of Russian Vitebesk, has that same immeasurable breadth (the *širokaja natura*), and the abstruseness of the petit bourgeoise milieu in his works is also suffused with Hasidic wisdom much like the village milieu in the works of Chagall.

Also in Kafka's works a bouquet of flowers suddenly might become overly lifesize, a human being seems to be flying pellmell over the landscape (as a person, not in a balloon or airplane) or seems to be riding on peculiar forms through outlandish space, the household utensils enter into conversation with their owner, things and animals are inextricably bound up with the course of human life."

All of the above is no more than a parallel and yet as such is revelatory of the era and of Kafka as a child of that era. The name of Chagall does not occur at all and that of Paul Klee (1879–1940) is also missing in the well known notes of Kafka, although Klee definitely belongs to the Kafka-sphere by virtue of his universe of ideas as well as his expressive forms. I had occasion early in the twenties to ask Paul Klee, then in Munich, to place at my disposal a goodly number of drawings and aquarelles for the first Paul Klee exhibit in Prague which young Czech artists of my acquaintance wanted to set up. Klee sent me a lot of material, which was however highly insured and consequently aroused the suspicions of the Czech customs officer. But after looking the material over he let it go through customs duty-free on the grounds that, as he said, "my little boy paints things like that by the hundreds." And thus in utter innocence he established the quite pertinent connection with children's art and so saved us money. I assisted in hanging the pictures in the Rudolfinum exhibit hall but I can no longer recall whether Kafka ever got to see this exhibit. Certainly one can also observe correspondences to Kafka's world in the works of Odilon Redon (1840–1916) and especially in those of James Ensor (1860–1949). Ladendorf has reproduced Ensor's astonishing representation of a human being become insect, which as early as 1888 anticipated Kafka's famous tragi-grotesque motif of the transmogrification or metamorphosis. This find had something disturbing about itself.

I never encountered Kafka in the company or in the studios of the more or less cubist avant-garde Czech painters (Josef Čapek, Václav Špála, Vlastislav Hofman, Emil Filla, Jan Zrzavý, Rudolf Kremlička), with whom I had enjoyed a friendly association since 1916. At an exhibit he had learned to know Vlastislav Hofman's graphic cycle of figures derived from Dostoevsky's novels, somewhat cool and related to the woodcuts of the sculptor Josef Bílek, and I think I recall that he liked this cycle. Kafka approved of (probably excessively so) the sculptures of Josef Bílek, he actually venerated the St. Wenzel Monument in Prague's St. Wenceslas Square done by Josef Václav Myslbek (1848–1922), the Czech sculptor, whereas he regarded the remaining memorial sculptures in Prague (such as Ladislav Šaloun's statue of Hus in the Altstädter Ring) as mediocre and in certain instances downright bad. Among Prague painters Willy Nowak (to be classified according to descent somewhere between the Czechs and the Germans; he was the brother-in-law of Theodor Däubler) had distinguished himself by virtue of his colorful and gay landscape and genre painting. Kafka thought highly of Nowak's work and also acquired something from it.

As early as 1918 I had called attention in the Berlin review *Aktion* to the then nascent Czech art of the cubist avant-garde. Their efflorescence, however, did not actually commence till the twenties and hence extended into Kafka's purview only in an occasional individual work. In such cases his artistic judgment was just as clean and genuine as everything else about him. That he inclined to overestimate the sculptor Bílek may possibly be explained in part by the fact that this isolated artist, truly *sui generis*, reflected a felt affinity to the great symbolist Czech lyric poet of that time, Otakar Březina, whom we all venerated so greatly.

Though Kafka's own sketches must necessarily remain a "sideline" of the prose narrator and philosophical seeker, they are nevertheless related to his stories and his search and complement them in an extremely revelatory way. Such was the case also with Goethe, who—after deciding to renounce his plan to devote himself exclusively to painting—still continued regularly with his drawing not only because this enabled him to retain visually and thus to recall more easily what he saw and experienced but also because it afforded him the opportunity to interpret things in a medium other than the literary. Surely, Kafka would not have commenced the systematic study of art as a youth in school, if he had not suspected that art was an indispensable means of knowledge and expression for himself. This man, surrounded everywhere in his native city by works of great art, wanted to know precisely what really was going on round about him. That he did not, however, choose plastic art as his chief medium may perhaps be explained by the aforementioned "Hear, oh Israel" to which the spoken or written word, the perceptible statement, corresponds more adequately.

FK

11 JUNE 1924

Wednesday, 11 June 1924 dawned as a friendly morning in Prague. The city was already in summer's light and an accelerating vacation mood. The republic, under the aegis of wise Thomas Garrigue Masaryk, had already existed for five and a half years and appeared firmly established despite all inner conflicts and external problems. At all events the citizens of Prague had that feeling (including also the Germans among them). The historic city with its brilliantly sunlighted

roofs under which timeless national and religious contrasts cast their shadows prepared
to transfer from its morning pleasure to the
moderate diligence of a late spring day,
which as always would be redolent with the
emerald gorgeousness of the gardens as well
as constantly resounding the background
chords of Bohemian musicality, transfused
with the smell of smoked meats and beer, and
vibrating continuously with a growing national spirit of hostility toward evening.

The times were not exactly simple but
where were the times? In Italy the fascisti
were staging their dark machinations; but
then Italy was far away. In Russia Lenin had
died in January and Trotsky was banished;
but then Russia was also far away and be-
sides for some time now it was no longer the
all-embracing Slavic Little Mother of past
pan-Slavic days. In America Woodrow Wil-
son had died on 3 February and thus one of
the grand architects of the New Peace and
friend of Masaryk had passed away; nonetheless Europe again felt far, very far away
from America. In Germany a loud-mouthed
unknown was preparing to write a book called
Mein Kampf. But of what concern is Germany
to us? In Prague most girls were interested
in having bobbed hair which was just becom-

ing popular with women; an event of world importance, a tremendous innovation.

For the German literary artists and writers of Prague, particularly the German Jews of this city, 11 June was sad and painful. Franz Kafka had succumbed eight days earlier in Sanatorium Kierling in the Viennese Woods near Vienna to his long and tortuous suffering. His remains had been sent to Prague and now on this Wednesday he was to be buried. The servant of God, the aphoristician of prose seemed also to have compressed his life aphoristically. Actually his death struck his family, his friends, and acquaintances like a bolt of lightning and seemed incredible though most of them had known for a long time that his death was imminent. But all of us—including the literary artists among us, who from youth on had reflected on and poetized about death—were not up to its direct actuality within our circle. I alone had seen the young writer Brand die in his destitute home in Prague. The war had of course deprived us of relatives and friends and also another Prague German poet (the highly talented Franz Janowitz), but to us war was murder imposed upon man and his dear ones by man's own inhumanity. That was not death, not the one preordained by God, but rather an attack

on God. The German literary artists of Prague
including Kafka had never accepted humanly
determined extinction as "death" in any
proper sense.

Kafka had not yet concluded his forty-first
year. I am convinced that no one could have
known him personally without loving him.
And it must be said that all who loved Kafka
also loved the latter's friends for his sake,
and that he created an invisible bond between
all who felt they were in his everlasting presence, and that by virtue of his living and
doing they had become associated with something higher and better and thus were personally enhanced and sanctioned. This kind
of strengthening and affirming power had issued from Kafka. Should it now suddenly
cease to exist? At that time he was not "famous" in the customary sense of that word,
as some other citizens of Prague were. Outside of his Prague circle only the more profound knowers of literature, the limited number of talent seekers among publishers, editors, or other intellectuals cherished him. We
in Prague did, however, know who it was that
daily walked through our day in the old lanes,
who it was we greeted across the streetcar
tracks—indeed, a simple return greeting had
the effect of a special event—or who it was
with whom we walked here or there past a

few houses or sat down somewhere for an hour over a cup of coffee without his being at all loquacious (though every one of his sentences always and invariably, yes every casual word of his, penetrated down deeply to the very center of the earth). But no one could explain this penetration to the bowels of the earth, not even his equals, not even Max Brod, the clarifier and eternal stimulator; neither the philosophical Felix Weltsch; neither the idealistic religious scholar Hugo Bergmann; nor Oskar Baum, the writing Tiresias among us bereft of sunlight by a boy's toss of a rock but now able insightfully to peer into the rays of the soul. However, they did know how to explain what Kafka may have meant and one could agree with their interpretations or offer one's own. But how it happened that Kafka said what he said; how it happened that he said it the way he said it; how it happened that one never came into conflict with what he said or with him himself, that no one could explain. The fact of the matter was, however, bound up with another fact, namely, that Kafka was not a culmination but rather the beginning of a new era. And so a particularly profound anxiety on the part of us young literary artists accompanied his demise.

Werfel, who had been living far from

Prague for several years already and returned home only occasionally to visit, once
said to me: "I would love Kafka much more,
if he were not so nihilistic." Nihilistic! How
so? Seldom has a judgment as wrong as that
one been expressed though it did sound plausible coming from Werfel. The "we are" (*Wir
Sind*) and the "each other" (*Einander*) of
the friend of the world (*Der Weltfreund*)
were defending themselves involuntarily
against the inexhaustible and basic tragedy
of existence. There was nothing Danaidic
about Werfel, he believed—at least at that
time—in the possibility of the golden reconciliation, attempted—precisely at the time
Kafka was dying—the ultimate reconciliation
of the great contrapositions in Verdi and Wagner, in Juarez and Maximilian. All of us loved
the genius of Werfel's affirmation of the world
and his approval of life, for after all we all
wanted the world and life. Kafka also wanted
them. Indeed, no one fought as hard and as
despairingly as he did in their behalf, no one
took a position such as he did against the incessant disappointments and frustrations which
life, the world, and its inhabitants evidenced
to all who embraced them wholeheartedly.
Kafka was that kind of devotee, not a nihilist.
The enduring value of his masterfulness lay
in the teacher image of an incorruptible per-

ception of his own secret weaknesses with the result of fragmenting himself in every one of his works only to make another fresh start, that is, to humble himself once more by returning to the source.

But now he had departed us, and we were to bury him in the afternoon, in his "resting" place where "the dead are brought to rest." Wrong! They do not rest. Somehow the body returns to dust but what does that have to do with the eternal persistence of the spirit? We of his inner circle not only suspected but were certain of his greatness though certainly not all of us appreciated how effective and discernible his greatness would become. In the universe of German literature highly significant minds were still living and trying to create, people who had shared in giving a new face and a new vitality to this body of literature; both in the north, in a Germany suffering from inflation, as well as in the south, in a Vienna deprived of its ancient coordinates of existence, many literary hopes were still sparkling which were somewhat clumsily called "expressionist" for the sole purpose of evaluating them. Several of us Prague writers were included in this group, also Kafka. Despite that fact, we regarded ourselves as a unique congregation of proven purity with respect to our linguistic expression and tested in long-lasting experiences in the pro and contra of close symbiosis with the Slavs. Accordingly we were Germans of a special kind, Austrians of a special kind, Bohemians of a special kind, and most of Kafka's friends were in addition characterized still further by involvement with the peculiarities of Jewish problematics. His death now tore out the capstone of this congregation, broke its arch. Would it ever become whole again or would it collapse? Would the storms completely destroy the building? The rains came. The building collapsed.

In fact, the intellectual Prague of that Czech-German-Austrian-Jewish synthesis which had sustained the metropolitan aspect of the city and inspired it throughout centuries, came to an end with Kafka. The Czechs of that day were least aware of the foregoing, just as they had failed in general to take any but sporadic, inadequate, and almost indifferent notice of the intellectual labors of their German compatriots. We must mention a single exception to the foregoing at this point, namely youthful Milena Jesenská, who loved Kafka and also translated some of his shorter prose pieces into Czech. (She translated *The Stoker* for Stanislav Kostka Neumann's journal *Kmen* [1920]; also *The Verdict, The Metamorphosis*, and *Meditation*—Milena Jesenská also provided the only Czech obituary of Kafka in *Národní Listy*, a Prague daily, 6 June 1924.) Regarding this wonderful woman who went to her death in a German concentration camp, see Margarete Buber-Neumann's book *Kafkas Freundin Milena* (Munich, 1963). But almost all other literary Czechs were much better informed about mediocre French scribblers than about their German neighbors in the next street, regardless of whether they went by the name of Rilke, Kafka, Werfel, or Brod, though the latter did so much for the world understanding of Czech culture. This inattention of the Czechs at that time might seem understandable to a degree inasmuch as they were before all else still quite giddy, inebriated, and even overwhelmed by the sudden intrusion of political independence and by their confusing hegemony over other nations. And how could they then have suspected that the name of the German-Jewish writer, who was, generally speaking, scarcely known and who was to be buried that afternoon, would remain irrevocably associated with the viable name of their charismatic capital Prague? How could they have suspected ever so remotely that one day people all over the world would involuntarily react with "Prague" whenever they heard the mere mention of the name "Kafka," indeed, that this historic city of European importance would already within three decades acquire significance for countless numbers simply as the hometown of Kafka?

And yet—Kafka was Prague, and Prague was Kafka. It had never been so completely and so typically Prague, nor would ever again be so as it was in Kafka's lifetime. And we, his friends, "the happy few"—if such a designation is permissible on the day of burial— we knew, that this Prague permeated all of Kafka's writings in the most refined miniscule quantities. We could and still can say "Prague" with every line Kafka wrote despite the consolidation of his works from year to year to such an extent that they seem to have become independent of temporal and spatial relations. It is an almost satirical achievement of Kafka that the Prague which came to an end with him was not buried with him, though none, not even all those of the aforementioned "band of brethren," were aware of this fact at that time.

Every one rode or walked, each in his own way, to the Jewish cemetery of Strašnice, a suburb on Prague's periphery. The pleasant weather of the morning had meanwhile become cloudy. The majestic city with its towers and bridged river is no longer visible from the Strašnice plateau. Here the countryside

192

begins to spread out toward Bohemia and is reserved for the silent orders of the dead whose kingdoms begin earlier already in the north, if one can speak of mundane geography in connection with the dead. That Kafka should be laid to rest here was strange and incredible inasmuch as we were aware of his stronger being (*hic et ubique*) and knew that he would unexpectedly be meeting up with us in varying forms; the closer we got to the graveyard, the more we were divested of the feeling of finality. I walked in the cortege escorting Kafka's coffin from the ceremonial hall to the open grave; behind the family and Kafka's pale lady-companion, beloved Dora Dymant, supported by Max Brod, I walked with his friends. All of them were still young, though the oldest among them (Brod, Hugo Bergmann, and Oskar Baum) were in their early forties; Felix Weltsch, Ludwig Winder, Rudolf Fuchs, and Friedrich Thieberger (my brother-in-law and Kafka's Hebrew teacher) still in their thirties; I was twenty-nine. Only a few of the approximately hundred people then walking along among the meadows and cypresses are still living and could become witnesses of Kafka's paradigmatic world significance. As the casket was lowered, Dora Dymant let out a penetrating and painful cry, but her sobbing, which only he for whom it was intended could assess, died away in the echo of the Hebrew prayer for the dead, which proclaimed the holiness of God and the profound hope of salvation. "Writing as a form of prayer," that had been Kafka's definition of the writer; and "even if salvation fails to come, I want to be worthy of it every minute," that was his faith. We cast earth onto the coffin. I recall this earth exactly. It was light colored, lumpy, clayish, permeated with little stones and pebbles, which rumbled onto the box. Then the mourners disbanded. I walked away between the graves with my wife, who from childhood had been friend and neighbor to Kafka, and with the author and translator Rudolph Fuchs. Not a word was spoken. Finally the darkened sky even gave forth rain. ["Endlich fing es gar aus dem trüb gewordenen Himmel zu regnen an." (Kafka, *Betrachtungen*)]

Eight days later (19 June, 11 A.M.) the memorial service for Kafka took place in the "Kleine Bühne" ("Little Theater"), the German chamber theater of Prague at that time. Credit for arranging the service and preparing the hall belongs to the Prague lyric poet and dramaturgist Hans Demetz, father of the literary scholar Peter Demetz now living and working in the U.S.A. The hall with a capacity of about 500 was completely filled almost exclusively by German-speaking Jews of Prague. This is not to say that the Czechs or non-Jewish Germans of Prague purposefully stayed away. But the name Kafka carried little weight with them at that time. The publishers Kurt Wolff and Ernst Rowohlt had recognized Kafka's importance as early as 1913, that is, more than a decade ago; *Meditation, The Stoker, The Metamorphosis, The Verdict, A Country Doctor,* and *The Penal Colony* had appeared and anyone with an ear for literature had an idea of what was going on. But as always most people had their ears cocked in quite different directions. For many of these non-hearers the phase of compulsory feeling came only later on. As the German proverb has it: "Wer nicht hören will muss Fühlen."

After some introductory remarks by Hans Demetz, who spoke also in his capacity as co-founder with the poet Hans Regina von Nack of the Prague German "Literary and Artistic Society," Max Brod presented his great eulogy. He was the oldest and closest friend, the most reliable person who knew Kafka the man. He was a native of Prague, who himself had chosen Prague for the locale of his novels, and who could conjure forth Kafka's image from its very own primal world and as a profound mirror of this world.

But even more: He was and is the spirit to
whom the world owes the author Kafka, his
true father, who launched Kafka on his labyrinthine path happily yet painfully and with
an incomparable self-effacement. One can
speak of him, who became eighty in 1964,
only with the greatest veneration, and only
those who personally participated in the German literary life of Prague at that time can
estimate the enormous stimulation he provided. All the more regrettable is the fact
that his eulogy at Franz Kafka's *nekyia* has
been lost. He spoke of Kafka's future, of an
approaching Kafka-era that would recognize
him as a constructive assessor of the basic
nature of mankind which manifests its weaknesses and inadequacies contemporarily. In
these terms he regarded him as being what a
literary artist should be, namely, as a monitor
"the attitude of him cheers up slaves and hor-
rifies foreign despots" (Walt Whitman), and
as being what all great prophets have been
upon whose mystic union with their community the splendor of *Shekinah* shone, the presence of God among men.

It was given to me to speak after Brod on
behalf of the younger generation of literary
artists. And I too had chosen as my theme—
quite independently of Brod—the idea of
Kafka's living on and of his profound and

extensive influence. And so this necro-eulogy actually become a celebration of life and most properly so in a religious sense, for just as Jews call the graveyard "the house of life," we who had buried him and those other friends present at that ceremony insisted that he should remain and be what he was. In his autobiography *Streitbares Leben* (1960) Max Brod mentions a newspaper clipping recalling that Hans Hellmuth Koch, an actor with the "Prague German Theater," following upon the eulogies of Brod and myself, read aloud the cemetery scene *A Dream* and finally *An Imperial Message*, which he concluded in whispers as a result of overwhelming emotion.

In 1959—that is, thirty-five years after that solemn hour—the publisher Hartfrid Voss of Ebenhausen near Munich approached me, who at that time had been living in New York for eighteen years, with the request that I provide him with a copy of my eulogy of Kafka—for inclusion in a book to be entitled *Unsterblicher Genius* (*Immortal Genius*) which was intended to renew the remembrance of German literary artists in the necrologies of their friends. Max Brod's eulogy was lost and could not be reconstructed. However, I too no longer had a copy of mine. I had left it behind in Prague in 1939 when I fled. Yet I recalled that Paul Westheim had published

a substantial portion of it some months after
its delivery in his journal *Das Kunstblatt* in
Berlin. But I also no longer had an offprint
of that publication. However, the Library of
Congress in Washington once again came to
my aid, as it has done so often, by locating
my eulogy and sending me a photocopy of
it. It was an extraordinary sight again after
so many years and distant places. Today I
might have said some things differently from
the way I once did as a youth; but my recognition of merit still prevails today—*post tot
discrimina rerum.* My words of yonder day
are included in the book I have cited, which
also appends as a substitute for Max Brod's
lost eulogy a later memorial statement com-
posed by him, to which in view of the nature
of his relation to Kafka a special preference
must be accorded.

FK

MEMORIAL EULOGY

The text of my eulogy delivered at the memorial service for Kafka in Prague was
slightly longer than the version subsequently
published in the Berlin *Kunstblatt*. I can no
longer recall exactly what the editor deleted.
The suggestion of Kafka's future greatness
and effectiveness, so self-evident today, may
at that time not have sounded so convincing
to many people.

IN MEMORIAM FRANZ KAFKA

"I see gathered together here the friends
and admirers of a man and a literary artist
whose highest human quality simultaneously
produced his most powerful poetic magic. In
any case, if ever there was a perfect instance
of the congruence of life and artistry, it ap-
plies to Franz Kafka. This extraordinary man
created as he lived, in the self-chosen hard-
ships of a heartfelt prose made possible by
the involuntary modesty of genuine discern-
ment. The life of such men is fully appreciated only by those closest to them. Their
death, however, unites dispersed people, their
death in no wise represents something negative but rather a great fact of the spirit-
intellect, a nucleus of mysterious and ever
cumulative solidarity.

"How could we better do obeisance in the
presence of a phenomenon, which knew from
truth, purity, and ingenuousness how to build
throughout its life, except we ourselves become aware of our own conscience through
the instumentality of this presence? How can
we, a generation of very unstable values,
carry away with us more viably and lastingly
this model thrusting itself so powerfully upon
us except by making it an effective part of
ourselves? At the very moment the remains

are being removed from us and entrusted to inscrutable depositories a new and better heart seems to be growing for us in our attachment to this dead man. This fact perhaps represents some of the sense, wisdom, and comfort acquired from this departure.

"The truth, revered friends, is at home only where spirit-intellect and life are unable to operate without each other. They fail almost completely to correlate as regards most of us though they may do so partially in the case of a few. But only where the qualities of human nature are intimately related to the qualities of style, only there is it possible to lend credence to that style. . . . A human being should not include within himself an artist, nor should an artist include within himself a human being. Only when the two contours cohere does the word become flesh.

"Franz Kafka was a fanatic of the truth within himself. We know, there is not a single decorative line in his entire works, no forced smiling about his precious prose in its totality, no calculated pomp. The recurring fragmentariness of his creativity bears witness to us of his compulsion to the truth. Because he wrestled with his projections for truth's sake, he destroyed them; he destroyed them because he wanted to reveal their innermost being, their inner truth. . . . And so it seems to me, he had only a single brother: Kierkegaard —and only a single guideline, namely, that only he who persists till the end can become blessed.

"Today a few still realize what a master departed from us in Franz Kafka, and there is scarcely anyone in the realm of our contemporary German literature sufficiently neighborly to thank Kafka for his gift to her—indeed, it is questionable whether she is even aware of his gift to her. . . . And so we must continue to wait till those delicate organs sprout again which are necessary for apperceiving profundities and excellencies. . . . In our day Knut Hamsun might possibly be able to render thanks to this noble but unpretentious and modest but great literary artist who in a modern sense aroused our pleasure in antiquity. I can think of no one else.

"Of this I am sure, however, that about and around the work of the wondrous genius of Franz Kafka acclaims of veneration and love will accumulate more and more and that this legacy will with unifying power continue to attract all men of goodwill."

FK

CONCERNING THE DESTRUCTION
OF CREATIVE WORKS
BY THEIR CREATOR

In the thirteenth chapter of *The Life and Achievements of the Renowned Don Quixote de la Mancha,* Cervantes tells about the burial of the poet Grisostomo who worried himself to death because of his love for the shepherdess Marcella. This is no mere recounting of an imagined fable but rather a parable representing as a symbol (in Goethe's sense) all that happens but which also, though it expresses its content completely, yet points simultaneously to something higher. Thus, we may see in the lovely shepherdess Marcella life itself with all its temptations and vanities, and see in the poet Grisostomo the soul constantly longing for the meaning of life, a soul wishing to be accepted by life and to exist therein *dans le vrai,* but destroying itself as a result of its very desire for happiness, which is in essence extremely simple and yet utterly unattainable.

Round about the dead man's bier, under the escort of his many grieving friends and of a knight and his page and of some other casual attendant by the name of Vivaldo, lie the books and the posthumous manuscript remains of the deceased, who has sternly charged his best friend Ambrosio with the task of committing his literary estate to the fire at his burial. The bonfire has been prepared and the grave stands open. Ambrosio proceeds to eulogize his dead friend. He describes his virtues, his spirit and mind, his noble ethics, his social graces and the genuineness of his friendship. Heaven had graciously bestowed on Grisostomo an infinite measure of its richest gifts. He was not only the most perfect of men in the practice of everything good but also uniquely exemplary in bearing all manner of misfortune. He had loved with all his being but had been rejected. "He sought compassion in blocks of marble; he wanted to embrace the lifeless air; he listened for an echo from the soundless desert." Whereupon Ambrosio concludes the eulogy of his poet-friend with the assurance he could document the full measure of Grisostomo's love from the manuscripts heaped up alongside the grave and destined for all nations of the world in memory of the great passion, were it not for the fact that the author of these manuscripts had sternly and emphatically charged him to destroy the documents after his burial.

Ambrosio is interrupted at that point in his address by the aforementioned Vivaldo, who was attending this macabre service amidst the beautiful mountain landscape in the company of Don Quixote. Vivaldo obviously feels an ideological obligation to interfere at this point and prevent the loss of an invaluable something or other which, though he knows nothing about it, appears according to Ambrosio's indications to have far-reaching importance. "If you were to burn these papers," says he, "then your action would be more austere and more merciless than that of the deceased. For it is neither just nor sensible to give rein to the will of a dead man when his requests transgress the boundaries of the intelligently permissible. Would Caesar Augustus, for example, have been right, had he punctiliously carried out the last will and testament of Virgil, the divine Mantuan, by having the *Aeneid* burned? And even though you must let the corpse sink into the earth, you should nonetheless not commit the writings of the living to oblivion, for it is not seemly to accede thoughtlessly to the request of the poet resulting from discontent." And to add emphasis to his interference, Vivaldo continues: "Consider that you may just now be according these inscriptions their complete existence and that you can thereby bring it about that Marcella's (that is, life's) gruesomeness will live on in the memory of all generations, so that in times to come an example may have been provided to mankind of what they must avoid to prevent their falling into similar abysses. For Grisostomo's fate can teach us the end that must befall all who ride about wildly at full speed on senseless detours." And then Vivaldo undertakes to speak in the name of all those present and concludes with the words: "We beg of you, Ambrosio, to be sensible and to desist from your intent to burn these papers." While saying this, Vivaldo lifts up one of the manuscripts bearing the title *Song of Despair*. His intercession moves Ambrosio to recant at least a little inasmuch as he does preserve a packet of papers while consigning the remainder to flames.

Thus far Cervantes, from whose works, to be sure, many connecting lines to Kafka can be drawn, not only from, let's say, *Don Quixote* to *The Castle,* but also from the *Novellas Exemplares* (e.g., *Story of the Gypsy Girl*) to the operatic character Carmen, so beloved of Kafka; or even from the grandiose *Conversation of the Two Dogs of the Ascension Hospital at Valladolid* to the *Investigations of a Dog.* Recall, for example, the social criticism of the dog Berganza, who says there: "Who can repress badness? Who has the power to open men's eyes and to show them that the defenders are in actuality the aggressors, that the waking are asleep and that he to whom one gives his confidence is in truth a robber and one who kills his protector?" Whereupon the dog Cipion responds with realistic dryness: "You are absolutely right." Parenthetically, I should like to interpolate here that Kafka, who had had it especially after *The Truth about Sancho Pansa* (title of one of his aphorisms), was convinced that he recognized the page as the real motivating force of the novel and a highly contrived symbol. Accordingly, Don Quixote is the "devil," Sancho's daemon of which he must rid himself, and thus he becomes the chief purveyor of the dreadful knightly romances which turn the Don's head. Hence, it is Sancho who instigates the knightly follies, in which he then participates from a certain feeling of guilt, patiently but also amusedly. Thus the author Cervantes, his creature Sancho, and Don Quixote's world effected by Sancho constitute a unified creative system wherein tragic parodies reciprocate and at the same time parody each other. Hence, not only does the creator produce his creation, but the latter in turn develops the medium which retroactively keeps the creator himself alive, a circle operating parodistically and grotesquely by virtue of the very fact that it is a vicious circle. The speeches about the corpse and the literary estate of Grisostomo are the parodistic metaphors, not to be taken lightly, of this tragi-grotesque piece. The vicious circle could be resolved only by suicide, which would be represented by the destruction of the manuscripts. The spiritual suicide imposed upon the friend for indirect realization follows after the physical one which can of itself not suffice.

The report about the fate of Grisostomo's manuscripts is not cited here for the purpose of attempting to vindicate Max Brod as the executor of Kafka's last will and testament, for he requires no justification as regards the history of culture or of literature. Perceptions and observations on the part of human geniuses have an open character inasmuch as the

genius is not its own private property. "I did
not make myself," Goethe declared. Matter,
attacked since the day of the church fathers
as the possession of individuals, might perhaps from that point of view be subject to
controversy; but not genius. One does not
"acquire" it and, therefore, does not possess
it in the sense of property. At all events, the
problem of private control over spiritual-
intellectual bequests, insofar as one may regard it a problem, has been disputable for
ages, and that is precisely what Cervantes
emphasizes in his reference to Virgil. Particularly noteworthy with respect to his history
is the circumstance that Grisostomo's literary
estate is removed from the sphere of personal
prerogatives and its paradigmatic significance
worked out generally also for the future, that
is to say, its actual basic value. Cervantes is
speaking *pro domo* there inasmuch as his entire narrative work, even though it might incidentally culminate in amusing the reader
—and we say "amusing," not entertaining,
since the muses and not burlesque absurdity
thereby enter the picture—was obligated to
a critical-moral daemon into whose service
the author placed his depth psychology, not
of the contemporary or Spanish kind but
rather that of mankind in general.

It is unavoidable, of course, that every author should remain ambivalent toward every one of his works, indeed, to every one of his sentences, simply because every definition of phenomena—and the simplest story consists of such definitions—carries its own contradiction within itself and consequently also casts its grotesque metaphysical shadows, to disregard which would signify a distortion of the inner truth (also characterize an inadequate narrative style). A reflective and responsible writer cannot assume a dictatorial stance toward and pertly determine the phenomena of the world and of life: "That and that are thus and so, and not otherwise; *Roma locuta, causa finita.*" For he knows very well that he is really everywhere and continuously engaged in the process of investigating phenomena and each of his works always constitutes no more than a phase of his never-ending mission exposed to the most contradictory and unconjectural adventures. If he publishes a work then he can in good conscience say at best: It has got this far till now. The significance of his work for his readers then 'depends in good measure on the amount of trust they accord him. His life and his personality are accordingly and without doubt also a part of his work. And the implication of more recent literary research that the biographical data of a literary personality can be separated from his work, which is the sole arbiter of the knowledge and significance of the created product, is in error.

Now, it is, of course, always possible that an author because of the crisscrossing of the lines of his research may take off into a surprisingly unexpected direction. The resulting contradiction may be part of a development and need not be judged unconditionally as characteristic deterioration. For the author is not a static phenomenon, he is live, hence changeable. Within one and the same piece of work it is even possible for him to establish mutually incompatible determinations and yet be correct as regards the whole. A single personality consisting of nothing but negative characteristics could nonetheless function virtuously as a total manifestation; and a person achieving good in a thousand individual cases might still in his totality be worthless. Accordingly, the conscience of an author is always suffused with doubts, he is filled with uncertainty and his attitude toward his work remains ambivalent, and not only respecting his style. Indeed, the restriction "not only respecting his style" is really not at all permissible, because the two, style and content, are inseparable. Consequently, if someone has doubts about his style and his work, he is doubting himself and his innermost being. However,

the author himself never knows with complete
certainty how significant the irradiations of a
book or even a sentence or a neologism really
are. For all of these are dependent upon temporal and spatial assumptions, upon the ability of the reader to comprehend, in short,
upon variable and cyclically conditioned factors which can effect changes in meaning. Yes,
language itself, the unique language of the
literary artist contains within itself changing,
deepening, or externalizing powers which are
active in connection with a viable willpower
and can enhance or diminish an insight or a
demonstrable phenomenon in such a way as
to leave the author utterly powerless regarding them. No word-symbol or sentence structure, even of a unique language, ever corresponds fully to some imagined, thought out,
sensed, felt, experienced thing, and it is a
commonplace that—to use only two basic
words—*love* and *freedom* signify something
different in every one of the countless languages and variant dialects of the earth,
though they may have a common meaning for
dolts and empty-heads. Thus, when persons
living outside the pale of creative literature
(or art of any kind) insist that the creative
artist achieve an act of independent will by
means of his work, then such insistence is no
more than a naive supposition. I have in mind

212

here not just the at times annoying, ludicrous, silly, or childish attacks of some kind of political, moral, or other censorship. I am talking about the relationship, unmodified by any kind of temporal externalities, of the author to his work during the genetic process thereof. In this process less personal free-willing and less possibility for some kind of choosing are present than in all other kinds of human endeavors or attitudes. And it is precisely this condition that exiles the literary artist or writer (and I do not have in mind the poetaster or would-be-poet) to his utterly lonely isolation from all other men. The exigencies of external compulsion, whether they be of a professional or political kind, family-conditioned illnesses and "ignoble misfortune" (Max Brod's phrase) may oppress the author just as they do any other person and they may restrict the freedom of his decisions literally to the customary minimum. Above and beyond all that, however—and that is his unique destiny—he is still with all his "being completely free" subject to indefinable necessities, liable to undocumented laws, accused by the secret courts of style and language, these latter being used all the while by all the other people in casual and obvious ways. A run-of-the-mill uninformed person conducts pedestrian transactions in the language of Goethe

or Hölderlin or is at least inclined to think
it is the same language, and precisely therein
lies the cleavage, therein lies the error.

Only pedestrian logic presupposes that the
artist will follow his preconceived blueprint
and ultimately realize an intended plan or at
least approximate it. But the work of art, like
man himself, has a destiny definable in only
a very limited way in terms of the person,
and an incalculable *moira* sways about over
this destiny and so it may occur—indeed, it
occurs often, and certainly it did happen in
connection with the larger intentions of Kafka
—that the work of art develops not only independently of its creator but diametrically
opposite to his intention. Here lies one of the
chief reasons for the author's ambivalence
toward his work, an ambivalence which in
Kafka's case, but not only in his, can culminate in certain moments in the will to destroy,
just as Cervantes' report about Grisostomo's
manuscripts indicates. And when Goethe reports to Eckermann (30 March 1824), as I
have already indicated earlier: "I did not
make myself," and even underlines this stric-
ture by adding that Shakespeare also did not
make himself, he thereby emphasizes the autonomous character of the work of art, which
nonetheless remains identical with its creator
just as the image of God does in relation to

God, although the author can decide to reject the work despite his having created it. This is precisely the conflict and the source of the unavoidable torture of ambivalence.

One need not be a Kafka to suspect that in every man, in every thing and, generally speaking, in every entity there are more reservations and secrets than unconcealed revelations. One can easily surmise all that but it can be known only with difficulty and, at best, only fragmentarily; furthermore, this kind of fragmentary knowing is probably one of the reasons for the fragmentation of expression as well as for the fact that the power of a work of art or of even a single sentence to carry conviction may reside less in what is actually said than in what has been withheld, and thus the essence of what has been reserved and hidden can stand in direct opposition to what has been revealed. This is why the artist's vocation is so hard, so dangerous, and so labyrinthine. And consequently the authors who have undergone profound poetic creative experiences incline to advise young literary adepts against traversing these labyrinths. For it is one thing to write down a complete sentence, to structure a character, to motivate an event with inexpressible pleasure but quite another thing to maintain all that in perfect sensuous balance with the totality of human existence and not let the Ariadne-thread of return slip away. The very idea: I cannot return, I and my projections might forever be separate from the whole world—possibly just because I have limned this world too sharply and too candescent clearly—this idea is the fourth Erinys, mythologically undocumented, the prime persecutor of literary artists. Conversely, the difficulties of an author with publishers, critics, the public and such, are unimportant "ignoble" misfortune devoid of any real significance.

Neither painful content nor personal suffering—be it of love or of bodily ills or of the conflicts of indecision—would invalidate the proposition that Kafka created with zest. Whoever might sense a masochistic self-torture in Kafka's creative processes is in error, and this least of all because of the humor or irony which coruscate in the parabolic aspect of his projection. All creativity deviously consists of excising an element of order from chaos, whereby chaos is, however, not completely negated; on the contrary, proof seems to have been presented to support the assumption that chaos possibly contains an element of order. The reverse process might also appear to be legitimate. But the creative process that achieved the tortures of Macbeth,

216

or the one that structured the sufferings of the Brothers Karamasov, do not represent a painful condition but rather the transfiguration thereof. It is in this sense that the story of the gate guards or that of the imperial message, which give painful expression to the nearly untranslatable or inadequately and "vainly" designated concept of "frustration"—just like the greater part of the remaining works of Kafka—are nonetheless written with immeasurable creative gusto. Not perhaps because Kafka had partaken with pleasure of the torture of his prospective readers, but joyous in the realization: "Now I've brought the matter out into the open! Thus and in no other way does existence run its course! I have tracked down the primal phenomenon (*Urphänomen*)!" Nor are the ever and ever renewed renderings, the recurring revised versions of the same theme, the never-ending polishing and correcting of rough sketches, a torture but rather a new embrace and lovemaking, a passionate longing to sustain viability. Only that which one no longer touches remains rigid and statuesque; life continues pulsating only where one is convinced that changes ought continuously to be made. And when an author cannot escape from his theme, when he repeatedly returns to working on it and illuminating it from all sides, when he cannot bring it to a close, this obviously proves only how immeasurably he loves it. If he should "suffer" in this process, then his pains are the passion of love to which even the happiest of lovers is unavoidably exposed.

The question remains moot whether love is sufficient, whether the lover is satisfied, whether the great transfiguration has succeeded, and whether one is the chosen one to complete it. What author of responsibility could escape this ambivalent doubt?

Neither Flaubert nor Ibsen escaped it, not even Goethe, the declared "favorite of the muses and graces," to name but three powerful literary personalities. However, we must also keep in mind the well-founded fears about the destiny of the work of art as regards its consumers and the destiny of the readers upon whom the work descends like a veritable stroke of fate. Abuse and misinterpretation in connection with such prime authors as Schiller, Hölderlin, Stifter, Nietzsche, or George, cower in the background of such considerations. It could, indeed, be said that it were almost a sign of insignificance to gain unexceptionable approval or to fail to be misinterpreted by the amateurs or malevolents. Intellectual property roves and like currency gets into the hands of the deserving as well as the unworthy (most of it goes to the latter) and is applied less to essential and meaningful matters than to superficial and nonsensical things. Likewise, intellectual property is stolen, invested, and embezzled. And though the latter might well be the lesser evil, less certainly than the allegation of the baser metals of mediocrity, the author can easily develop a real anxiety about everything he ever said or even just thought, indeed, even about his own hopes and dreams which he has even clothed with the power to revolt violently against oneself. And the person who believes in eternity and regards physical death not primitively as being *end sans phrase* he may have cause to shudder all the more about his literary estate in proportion to its significance. It will remain indelible, however, that Kafka emphasized in his diaries (8 February 1912) the net result of his studies of Goethe with the latter's sentence: "My pleasure in creating was boundless."

Though the majority of what Kafka actually recorded is also part of the literary legacy he left behind, he had published more, as he saw his end approaching, than people are usually aware of. However, nothing is more annoying to a writer than to see or conjure up his already published writings, the

urgent reminder of all that is apparently concluded, definitive, and irrevocable. For even
if recalling were possible and were to be
realized, it also would not be perfect or more
plausible than the first version, nor would it
be safe from further recallings. The idea of
the definitive character of what has been
published is all the more disturbing because
no one knows better than the author himself
the inhering fragmentariness of every statement. This feeling of fragmentariness causes
his isolation amidst all acceptance, recognition, and fame. But whoever might think that
Kafka attained to no "fame" during his lifetime is mistaken. He was, to be sure, not
famous in the sense of that Kafka who today
makes famous most of his interpreters. Kafka
in that image never really existed, or at least
only in minimal terms. But this living person-
age possessed the indefinable criteria of self-
evident fame and unconstrained significance,
unneedful of literary corroboration, a quality
which without exception everyone sensed who
knew how to read him or even came into
personal contact with him for as little as three
minutes of casual conversation on the street.
Conversely, I am convinced that, had Kafka
lived to experience his fame of today, he
would have stood his ground, inasmuch as the
three Erinyes of the compulsion to recogni-

tion, insatiability, and megalomania, which
ordinarily accompany fame, would have influenced him not at all, and inasmuch as he
never strove for that literary zenith from
which there is no return except complete collapse. For one does not fall slowly, one
plunges.

People have, almost customarily, again and
again called Kafka's prose masterful, though
occasional objection has been made to his
manner of speech, to an occasional Czech accent, and to occasional lapses into Czech-
Prague idiomatic turns. This is no place to
undertake comparisons with similar lapses of
accent or of idiom in the writings of other
significant writers of German prose, not only
in the various border areas in the east, south
or west or in the northern coastlands but also
in the central areas of the German-speaking
region. Kafka would stand out also among the
"best Germans." And elsewhere in this book
I have already discoursed about the intrinsic
values of Prague German. Meanwhile, prose
becomes masterful only when it is a prose of
ideas, when in truth every word, even a simple copulative, an adverb or a pronoun, let
alone a substantive or a verb, is an idea.
Only such a condition can culminate in form.
Genuine poetic language operates exclusively
in the abstract; it can contain no mere ex-

ternalities. Prose devoid of felt experience and thought is immediately recognizable by virtue of the fact that only verbs and nouns have a real function, and that all the other words appear lifeless and inserted solely as supports or connectives. The result is that the whole sentence fails to pulsate and seems instead to be manipulated like a puppet. It comes to life only if the puppeteer (the reader) decides to pull the strings. Even the most insignificant detail of the living body of a sentence (just as of the living body of a human being) is important, and if it is unhealthy, the entire body is affected. One must, however, always and at the same time keep in mind that every word also reflects those secret components lying back of its denotation which produce its immediate communicative effect, and this effect can on occasion signify the very opposite of the denotation. Hence, Kafka's statement that every line he writes is perfect must be regarded as a sign of his ambivalence rather than of linguistic self-confidence. I say "rather than," because this phrase has two aspects of which the second corresponds to the natural knowledge of one's own status which the thinking person "holds up as a shield" to his doubts, a shield he uses if he is not timid. And Kafka was humble though not faint-hearted, just as he was high-spirited but not haughty.

Obviously, irony even in its customary form is also a symptomatic component of ambivalence and constitutes a temporary means of escaping small as well as significant confrontations against which one might otherwise be helpless. There is no such thing as an ironic note separable from the reflecting subject. Every attitude can become comical or grotesque and hence the object of irony or satire by virtue of the conscious separation of the attitude from its authentic connections or from its otherwise established syndrome, the irony or satire thus emphasizing isolations of that kind by underlining them. Kafka's irony, however, penetrates more deeply beneath the merely harsh discrepancy of the contrasts by referring to the existence of the phenomena as such, which then appear disparate and vain simply because of their very presence, much like original sin, and indeed also because they would prefer to subsist simultaneously as both isolated and correlated but yet can never attain that condition. Therein lies the maximum tragedy but also the maximum eccentricity of Kafka's irony. On that high level of reflection, however, the balancing becomes nigh impossible for the observer, because this level is already on the extreme periphery of the abstract and he must consequently from this vantage point become dubious and ambivalent toward the creative process which led him to this height in the first place and now additionally superimposes self-irony on irony in the face of the phenomena.

Let us return to the "ingenious" Hidalgo Don Quixote, who probably represents the highpoint of all irony in the prose literature of all nations and who is commonly interpreted to mean that people become derisive in believing they are following high ideals by desiring to apply past and dead matters to viable and contemporary ones. But so-called "healthy" human common-sense rather than the "errant" knight becomes the subject of irony in this situation. For the knight fights in behalf of the pure ideas (in symbolic form) whereby man subsists as man and is justified; conversely, "healthy" *ratio* or mind is in the service of unwieldy *physis* or nature which seeks to refute the ideal with a heavy fist, that is, desires to dehumanize man and thereby liquidate him but in so doing *ratio* becomes derisive inasmuch as it also liquidates itself. The seemingly grotesque (that is, idealism) is in truth the serious business whereas the reasonable remains pitiable and inconsequential. That the knight as defender of the good and of the oppressed becomes a beaten up and derided victim is part of the business of wanting to be righteous, a desire consistently regarded as the acme of unrealistic foolishness. The Athenian who votes to ostracize Aristides, whom he does not even know, solely because he is annoyed that Aristides is commonly regarded as the "righteous one," is typical in this connection. People like Aristides are different from all those who accuse them of just wanting to be superior, simply because they are in fact superior. He who obeys the law instead of breaking it according to common custom is the real culprit.

Cervantes has his knight renounce all his follies as he lies dying, an act comparable symbolically to the obligation to destroy his ideological remains. But this renunciation has a hooker. For Don Quixote is well aware that he already has an executor, a writer, who has indicted a history of the knight's deeds, and that the latter's renunciation cannot eliminate or destroy the chronicle of his adventures long ago recorded and solidified. Accordingly, he formally asks pardon of his author and creator for having become the content and hero of his novel. Self-irony would thereby have achieved its very highest level, its most complete romanticism. Kafka was a realistic but also a romantic prose writer whose romanticism used manneristic metaphors of reality as a means of escape. Cervantes wrote *Don Quixote* in prison, a place—as he says—of unrest, sorrow, and misery. Franz Kafka did his writing amidst Europe and the configurations of life therein during the first quarter of this century and within the bureaucratic universe of an already bewildered burgherdom which felt itself to be safe solely within the iron bars with which it surrounded itself.

INDEX OF NAMES

Index

Professor Johannes Urzidil was born in 1896 in Prague and was in close contact with the Prague Literary Circle of Brod, Kafka, and Werfel. He has been a poet, novelist, journal editor, foreign correspondent, and translator (German to Czech), and has published stories, essays, and scholarly treatises. Among his better known and more important scholarly works are *Goethe in Böhmen* (*Goethe in Bohemia*), 1962; *Goethes Amerikabild* (*Goethe's Perception of America*), 1958; and *Amerika und die Antike* (*America and Ancient Antiquity*), 1964.

The manuscript was edited by Robert H. Tennenhouse. The book was designed by S. R. Tenenbaum. The typeface for the text is Bodoni Book based on the Bodoni face originally designed by Giambattista Bodoni in the 18th Century.

The book is printed on S. D. Warren's Olde Style Antique paper and bound in Interlaken's cloth over boards. Manufactured in the United States of America.